"Chefs have an emotional fascination with fire, something primal and intuitive. This is not chichi food. Michael's cooking comes from the heart, soul, and gut. Simple, straightforward, and convivial, it is the food of a true pitmaster."

—**JACQUES PÉPIN**

"Here's why I'm lucky . . . Michael Symon is my best friend and I've eaten most of the dishes in this book. I can smell the smoke and taste the fire of these recipes just by paging through the spectacular photos. The Fireplace Chicken has become legend in our friendship, and now it can all be yours."

—**BOBBY FLAY**

"I've long been a fan of Michael Symon—his genuine enthusiasm, wild talent, and love of food are evident in anything he touches. Over the years, I've watched him develop a deep love for and embrace the culture of barbecue. At Mabel's, he applied his immense skills to create a flavor profile that reflects his unique heritage and geography, and here he shares all that and more. In this book, readers can join his world and learn from one of the best as Michael offers his tips, tricks, and techniques for smoking meat. Anyone who loves barbecue will devour this book."

—**MIKE MILLS,** 17th Street Barbecue, author of *Praise the Lard* and *Peace, Love & Barbecue*

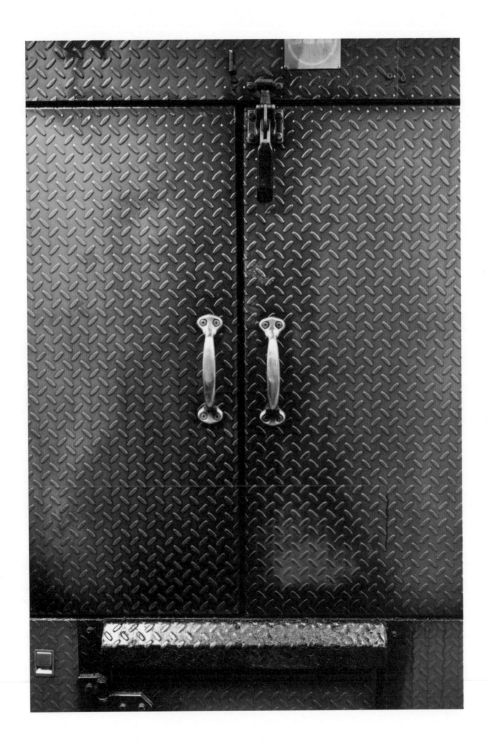

MICHAEL SYMON'S

PLAYING WITH FIRE

MICHAEL

PLAYING

Clarkson Potter/Publishers
NEW YORK

SYMON'S
WITH FIRE

BBQ and more from the grill, smoker, and fireplace

MICHAEL SYMON
and Douglas Trattner

Photographs by Ed Anderson

This book is dedicated to Lizzie, my lifelong partner, who grounds me, supports me, and inspires me to be a better person. I truly would not be here without you. Thank you, my vegetable-loving wife, for accepting and understanding my obsession with meat!

CONTENTS

My Love Letter to Live-Fire Cooking

Mabel's BBQ in Cleveland, Ohio, is a restaurant conceived from my life-long obsession with live-fire cooking. Whether it's grilling rib eyes, smoking lamb ribs, baking pizza in a homemade wood-fired oven, or just cooking hot dogs on a stick over a campfire, I have been in love with these primitive styles of cooking for as long as I can remember. So it's no surprise that for almost as long, I've been begging my business partners to let me open a barbecue restaurant. After close to twenty years of pleading, my wife, Liz, and business partner, Doug, finally relented, and in 2016 we opened Mabel's in downtown Cleveland.

My taste for barbecue came from my years of traveling around the country filming television shows like the Food Network's *Burgers, Brew & 'Que*, where I visited the country's absolute best barbecue joints and learned a lot about the various types of regional barbecue and the folks who make it. It quickly became apparent that all of the best pitmasters—regardless of where they happened to live and cook—prepared barbecue that was specific to their own particular region. That meant grilling or smoking indigenous animals over native hardwoods in equipment custom-built for that purpose. Everything from the cuts of meat and spice rubs to the sauces and sides is based on literally generations of local history, experience, and cultural preference.

That's why when the time (*finally!*) came for me to open up a barbecue restaurant of my own, I knew that I wanted to make it unique to my hometown. That meant crafting a style and menu that draw upon Cleveland's rich cultural heritage, much of which is firmly rooted in eastern Europe. We season meats with Jewish deli-style pastrami spices; our kielbasa is made by a sixty-year-old Ukrainian butcher at the West Side Market; we smoke over locally sourced apple- and cherrywoods; we serve Hungarian-based sides like spaetzle and cabbage; our tangy mustard-based sauce is designed around the legendary local stadium-style mustard Bertman Ball Park.

It's not that I don't love Carolina chopped pork, and Memphis dry ribs, and Kansas City burnt ends, and Texas hot links—I do, I love them all! But I had no desire to attempt to shoehorn one or all of those styles into my Cleveland restaurant. I wanted the sights, smells, and flavors to be reminiscent of the foods we grew up eating; otherwise, it wouldn't feel authentic. It wouldn't feel right.

And that's probably the most important thing that I picked up during all my travels. The BBQ folks who do it best, whether it's been for five years or five decades, have a genuine passion for the craft that comes straight from the heart. There's an obsessive dedication to step up their game every single day; to put in the work and time to make a brisket that is 1 percent better tomorrow than it was today. Despite their regional differences, barbecue pros—the true practitioners of low and slow—are all members of the same clan.

And I couldn't be more thrilled to join them and those who came before them. We've been blessed at Mabel's to have some of the biggest names in barbecue walk through our door and try our food. The response by them—and, more important, Clevelander diners—has been overwhelmingly positive. That tells us that we're doing something right and that this Cleveland-style barbecue just might have some legs after all!

GRILLS, SMOKERS, AND LIVE-FIRE CONTRAPTIONS

With so many different grills, pits, and smokers on the market these days, it's important for every pitmaster-in-training to carefully consider the pros and cons of each piece of equipment before making an investment. In addition to budget, the primary factors to consider are:

- How much space in your yard or patio do you have to play with?

- Do you want the equipment to be portable or fixed in place?

- How much time do you want to devote to tending to the cooking process?

- How many people will you typically be grilling or smoking for?

- What types of fuel do you intend to use: gas, electric, charcoal, or wood (chips, chunks, pellets, or logs)?

- Would you like the apparatus to do double-duty as a grill and smoker?

On the following pages, I've listed some of the most popular types of grills and smokers and which applications they tend to excel—and fail—at.

OFFSET SMOKER

When it comes to fantasies of becoming a world-class pitmaster, these beefy, fire-breathing beasts often play a starring role. Historically fabricated from repurposed oil drums or industrial-size propane tanks, these impressive cookers are utilized by some of the biggest names in American barbecue, from Billy Durney in Brooklyn to Kent Black in Lockhart, Texas. Offset smokers are also called stick burners because that is primarily how they're fueled. Heat and smoke are generated by a real wood fire in the firebox, which is offset from the main cook chamber, and move across the food and out through a tall smokestack. Properly handled, these devices produce the best quality barbecue around. Too bad they also tend to be large, heavy, expensive, and challenging to master. Some are so heavy, in fact, that you need to pour a concrete pad just to support them.

When shopping for an offset smoker, money buys you thicker steel, better welds, and superior design and construction, all of which assist in maintaining steady temps and, thus, producing better barbecue. Look for models with a baffle, a steel plate that helps to evenly distribute the heat throughout the cooking chamber. In addition to being great smokers, most offsets can do double-duty as a roomy charcoal or wood-fired grill.

- Ideal for wannabe pitmasters who have the time and patience to dedicate to true craft barbecue. It also helps to have the space and budget of a Texas oilman.

- Best suited to cooking any and every kind of meat, including brisket, pork butt, whole hogs, whole chickens, whole turkeys, and steaks and chops.

VERTICAL SMOKER

If you desire the ease of set-it-and-forget-it cooking, a vertical—or box or cabinet—smoker might be for you. Typically fueled by propane gas or electricity, these devices maintain a consistent temperature (high or low) with the push of a button or twist of a dial. Also, because they are tall and boxy, and feature multiple shelves, they can prepare a lot of food in a relatively small footprint. While some feature an offset firebox that can accommodate charcoal, wood, and wood chunks, most are heated from below and flavored only by wood chips, a deal-breaker for proponents of real barbecue who insist on live-fire cooking. Thick steel construction will cost more, but also will do a better job of maintaining consistent temperatures in less-than-perfect weather. Look for models with wheels if you'll be moving or storing the rig elsewhere in winter.

- Ideal for people who want the ability to smoke a lot of food in a small space without the hassle of dealing with wood or charcoal.

- Best suited to smoking ribs, sausage, turkey breast, pork belly, fish, and seafood.

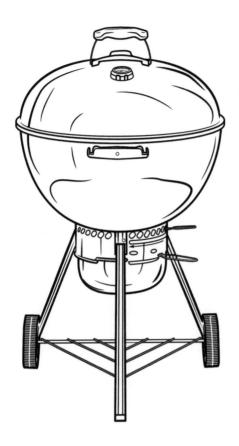

KETTLE GRILL

It seems like every household in America has a kettle grill, the most famous of which is the trusty old Weber. These charcoal-powered grills excel at cooking burgers and hot dogs on the Fourth of July, sure, but with a little know-how they can be converted into serviceable smokers, too. Using techniques such as the "snake" and "minion" methods (see pages 16–17), in conjunction with deft damper control, charcoal can be manipulated to burn very slowly over long periods of time. The addition of wood chips or chunks, often buried in the charcoal, add real smoke flavor throughout the cook. While they are fussy to smoke on, and they don't offer a ton of space in which to do it, they are affordable and portable, and you might already own one!

- Ideal for people who don't want to go out and buy another piece of equipment, but would like the option of smoking the occasional piece of meat.

- Best for cooking hot dogs and burgers, a couple racks of ribs, a whole chicken, sausage, and steaks.

WATER SMOKER

These charcoal-powered smokers look like a regular old kettle grill that got stretched out in the middle into the shape of a mini spaceship, fins and all. That expanded middle section is what makes these rigs so much better suited to smoking than their squat counterparts. That's where the water pan goes, which not only keeps the cooking chamber nice and humid, but also turns direct heat into the preferred indirect heat because it sits between the smoldering charcoal and the food. But the most useful advantage of that water pan is that it helps maintain ideal smoking temperatures in the 250°F range. Dampers above and below the cook chamber also help to modulate temperatures. These smokers can also double as a charcoal grill simply by removing the middle section, making them versatile. Like their kettle siblings, they have limited cooking space, so plan on keeping your barbecue bashes to a reasonable size.

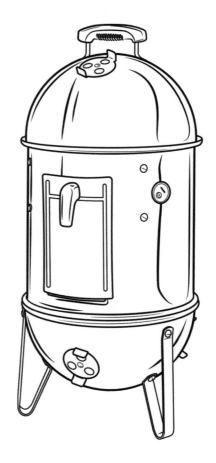

- Ideal for people who like the flexibility of a grill/smoker combo that doesn't take up a lot of space, is affordable, and can still turn out a pretty mean brisket.

- Best for cooking ribs, beef ribs, sausage, whole chicken, duck, and fish.

KAMADO

The Big Green Egg made this style of cooker popular, but it has since been joined by numerous brands and models that all feature the classic egg-shaped bodies constructed of thick-walled ceramic. Those dense earthenware walls are amazing at absorbing and maintaining heat, making these odd-looking contraptions outstanding smokers that don't require a lot of babying. Simply heat them up and close down the dampers, and they will coast for hours and hours at consistent temps. Though they look similar in appearance to regular kettle grills, these grills are considerably more versatile, capable of grilling a butterflied chicken, baking a thin-crust pizza, and smoking a meaty beef brisket. Now for the downsides: they tend to be expensive (anywhere from $500 to $2,000), very heavy, and cramped in terms of cooking area.

- Ideal for people who like the flexibility of a multipurpose grill and smoker, but don't have tons of outdoor space or the need to cook a lot of food at one time.

- Best for cooking almost anything, just not a lot of it at one time.

THE SNAKE AND
MINION METHODS

The typical method when firing up the old kettle grill or water smoker is to load up a chimney starter with charcoal, light it from below, and wait until all the coals are good and hot. At that point, all the glowing coals are dumped into the grill at once. The problem with this common technique is that the coals produce an intense amount of heat for a limited amount of time— roughly an hour or so—and then burn out. Since barbecue calls for lengthy periods of low to moderate heat, say, ten hours at 210°F to 250°F, the above situation is useless.

By employing techniques such as the "snake" and "minion" methods, home cooks can produce consistent temperatures over a very long time using regular charcoal and a standard kettle grill or water smoker. The two setups achieve the same goal but get there in slightly different ways. With the snake method, a low mound of just three or four unlit briquettes is arranged (like a snake) around the perimeter of the grill base. A small amount of hot, pre-lit briquettes is added at one end of the snake. The lit coals slowly and steadily ignite the adjacent unlit coals all the way down the line, producing a consistent, steady temperature. By placing wood chips or chunks on top of the unlit coals at regular intervals when setting it all up, you can also generate flavorful smoke throughout the entire process.

The minion method is the less fussy of the two setups. It starts by dumping a large amount of unlit briquettes into the base of the grill and then pouring a small amount of pre-lit briquettes right on top. The lit coals ignite the unlit coals beneath them, producing a steady supply of moderate heat. When setting this arrangement up, wood chips or chunks are buried into the pile at various intervals.

As with everything barbecue related, both methods require some tinkering and trial and error, especially when it comes to managing the dampers, or air vents, on the lower bowl of the grill. But when mastered, these techniques create the ideal environment for long smoke sessions without the need to constantly baby the process.

When using either of these methods, it's best to use "all-natural" briquettes like Stubb's All-Natural Bar-B-Q Charcoal (not to be confused with lump charcoal, which burns hotter and less evenly than commercial briquettes) because these products don't contain chemical binders that can contaminate the food. In normal grilling use, those binders largely burn off in the chimney starter before adding the coals to the grill.

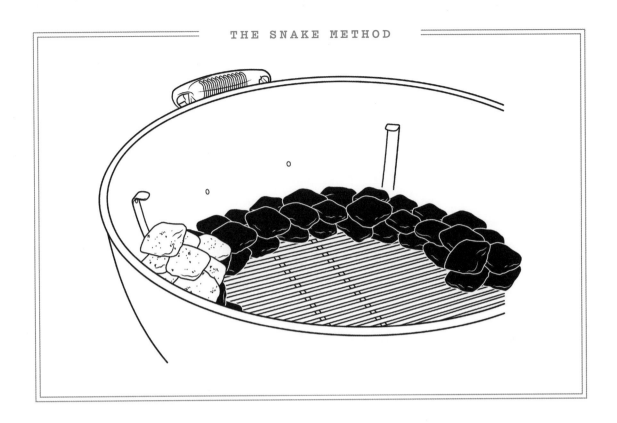

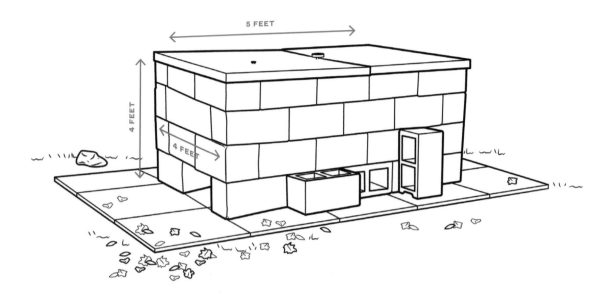

CINDER-BLOCK PIT

When it comes to cooking for a crowd—like thirty to fifty hungry guests—there is no beating the cinder-block pit, an apparatus ideally suited to—and likely conceived for—whole-hog barbecue. And the best part is that the entire grill can be constructed in very little time, for very little money, using common building supplies like cinder blocks from the local hardware store. Of course, your family and friends will probably think you're crazy to construct a 4 feet deep and 4 feet high by 5 feet long structure in the backyard, but wait until they dig into the succulent whole-hog barbecue! This ambitious project is great to tackle with a few like-minded friends over a long weekend filled with lots of cold beer that culminates in a barbecue for at least thirty people. Most of these rigs are fueled by hot coals, which are started in a fire burn pile nearby and shoveled into the pit at regular intervals to maintain consistent temps. You'll also want to fabricate a lid for that sucker out of corrugated metal roofing or sheet metal to retain heat.

- Ideal for people with tolerant spouses who enjoy DIY projects and want to build a large, possibly temporary, structure to feed a very large party.
- Best for cooking whole hogs, beef quarters, legs of lamb, mutton quarters, and massive quantities of burgers, steaks, and half chickens.

FIREPLACE

Even I have my limits when it comes to trudging outdoors and firing up the grill or smoker in the depths of another Cleveland winter. That's why fireplace cooking is one of the best inventions since the dawn of time. Not only do you get to stay inside, you get to stay inside by a roaring fire while watching your dinner cook! That said, this unconventional technique does require two things: a wood-burning fireplace and an understanding spouse who doesn't mind you cooking dinner in the living room. Lucky for me, I have both! Hearth cooking is surprisingly versatile in that you can cook foods directly in the coals—in a cast-iron pan on the hearth floor, on a grill grate perched above the embers, and by hanging a kettle or pot from a hook or from a string, and spinning it, rotisserie-style, just in front of the fireplace opening (pages 104–106 and 167). It might be a little messy, what with the occasional spattering fat, but it's fun, and it sure beats lacing up the boots!

- Ideal for people in cold climates (with well-trained dogs) who like to build fires and do things a little unconventionally.

- Best for cooking whole chickens, whole turkeys, and legs of lamb on a string, and anything that fits into a cast-iron pan, like beets, beans, and potatoes.

COOK TO TEMPERATURE, NOT TIME

Barbecue is a feel, not a formula. Given the amount of variables—type of wood, intensity of fire, size and shape of meat, even the weather—it's impossible to predict how long something will take to cook. That's what thermometers are for! Use them and you will almost certainly reach barbecue bliss.

A FEW WORDS ON BARBECUE

Barbecuing—and by that I mean the low-and-slow cooking of meats using live fire and smoke—is more art than science. Not that there isn't plenty of chemistry and physics going on, too, but I'm certainly not the guy to try to explain that stuff! What I mean to say is that the people who do it best have all gotten there by years of practice, trial and error, patience, and perseverance. Either that, or they grew up alongside someone who did so before them. Books and YouTube videos are helpful, but the best way to learn and perfect this art is to get out and try and fail and try again.

True barbecue is as much about building and maintaining fires as it is about sourcing, seasoning, and cooking meat. Which means that barbecue is also about buying, storing, and chopping wood, which is why so many home cooks opt for easier solutions like charcoal-fueled water smokers or gas- or electric-powered vertical smokers. But without live fire and real wood smoke, food will never reach its true potential to become that intoxicatingly flavorful, complex, and deeply aromatic food of the gods.

Pitmasters obsess over smoke: good smoke, bad smoke, black smoke, blue smoke. The goal is to create and maintain a steady flow of pale gray smoke that is so light, it almost looks blue. Throughout the book I instruct you to wait to place the food into the smoker until it reaches the proper temperature and "the smoke is running clear." This is the type of smoke I am referring to. Good smoke is produced by a properly built and tended fire burning at optimal temperature. Once that fire is going great, maintaining ideal cooking temperatures is as easy as adding an occasional log and regulating the airflow by adjusting the dampers.

To achieve that "good smoke," it's crucial to start with properly seasoned wood. Seasoned wood is wood that has been cut to length, split, stacked, and allowed to dry over months and months. Seasoned wood burns easier and faster and produces the kind of smoke that pitmasters require. You'll often hear barbecue pros go on and on about certain types of wood and how they are the best for this or that particular style or application of barbecue. But the one thing they all have in common is that they utilize species native to their location, because using what you readily have available just makes sense economically. In Texas, they burn post oak. In Kansas City, they burn hickory. In Cleveland, we burn apple- and cherry wood because northeast Ohio has tons of fruit orchards. Barbecue is regional because it developed around the use of local wood, livestock, and equipment.

I've never been the sort of chef who buys—or recommends that others buy—all sorts of cooking gadgets and equipment. I pretty much use two knives, a chef's knife and a paring knife, 90 percent of the time. So when it comes to barbecue gear, my list is pretty lean.

- Long-handled grill brush for scrubbing the grill grates

- Elbow-length heat-resistant gloves for tending fires

- Long, sturdy metal tongs for adding and removing food from the smoker

- Chimney starter for charcoal grills

- Instant thermometer for quickly checking the temperature of cooked or cooking foods

- Digital thermometer with leave-in probe for continuously monitoring the temperature of cooking foods without having to open the smoker

RESTAURANT TRICKS FOR HOME USE

One of the biggest challenges that a commercial barbecue restaurant faces that the home cook does not is holding fully cooked foods until they are ordered by a customer. At Mabel's, our smokers run around the clock, turning out pork ribs, beef briskets, giant beef ribs, and pork belly throughout the day and night. Managing the wrapping and holding of those meats so that they look and taste just as good when they are ordered as when they left the smoker is a complicated feat of technique, timing, and finesse.

Most commercial barbecue restaurants employ an expensive piece of equipment called a combination—or combi—oven, which maintains precise temperature and humidity levels to perfectly preserve the integrity of the food. I'm guessing you don't have one of these at home.

Here's the next best thing: When the fully cooked food comes out of the smoker, wrap it tightly in plastic wrap and then aluminum foil and place it in a well-insulated cooler or ice chest. There, it will hold beautifully for up to four hours. If you happen to have and prefer to use butcher paper like the pros, wrap the meat in that and place it into a cooler, but include a water pan or a damp towel for moisture.

True barbecue is as much about building and maintaining fires as it is about sourcing, seasoning, and cooking meat.

PORK

MABEL'S PORK BELLY

When it comes to cooking and eating, there are few things in this world that I love more than pork belly. This affordable cut of meat is so versatile. Most of us know that pork belly becomes bacon when it's cured and smoked. But when you simply season and smoke it, like we do at Mabel's, you end up with something completely different in texture. Our popular pork belly is smoky, meaty, and deliciously rich. Some might even say it's unctuous. How's that for a $10 word!

1 (10- to 12-pound) skin-off pork belly

1 cup Cleveland BBQ Sauce (page 220)

1 cup Pork Rub (page 234)

1. Prepare and preheat your smoker to 225°F.

2. Cut the pork belly crosswise into two equal pieces so it's easier to handle. Coat all sides of the pork with the barbecue sauce and then season it all over with the pork rub.

3. When the temperature in the smoker reaches 225°F and the smoke is running clear, add the pork belly fat-side up and cook until it reaches an internal temperature of 185°F, about 5 hours. For the best results, use a probe thermometer to continually monitor the meat's temperature.

4. Slice to the desired thickness and serve immediately, or hold for up to 4 hours according to the instructions on page 23.

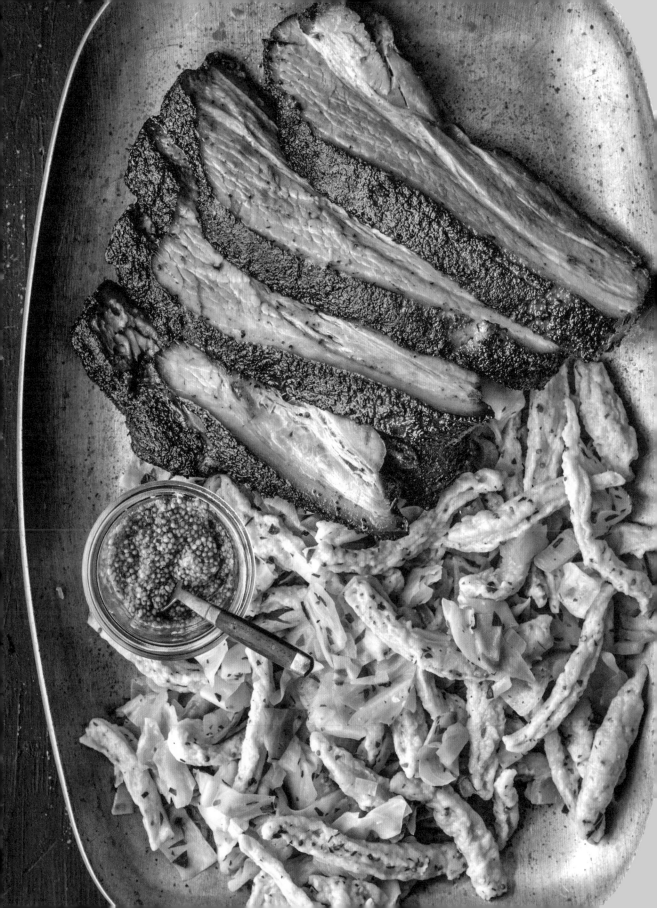

Be liberal with seasonings in order to achieve
deep flavor and develop that magical bark.

MABEL'S PORK RIBS

When it comes to pork ribs, nobody does them better than Mike Mills, who dominated the competition barbecue circuit for so long that he earned the nickname "the Legend" (see page 53 for his pork steak recipe). One of the biggest misconceptions about ribs is that they should be "fall off the bone" tender, but ask Mike and he'll tell you that "fall off the bone" is shorthand for "overcooked"! If you tried to pass those off to the judges at the world championship barbecue competition in Memphis, you'd quickly find yourself in the Losers' Lounge. Perfectly tender is a result we strive for every day at Mabel's. We also have a couple of secret weapons that make our ribs extra special: our rub has a good dose of flavorful celery seed, and as soon as the ribs come out of the smoker, we hit them with a pickle juice glaze, which gives them a nice punch of sweet and sour.

2 cups packed light brown sugar

1 cup strained dill pickle juice or sweet/hot pickle juice

2 (3- to 4-pound) slabs pork spareribs

1 cup Pork Rub (page 234)

2 cups Cleveland BBQ Sauce (page 220)

1. Prepare and preheat your smoker to 300°F.

2. In a large saucepan, whisk together the brown sugar and pickle juice. Heat over medium-high heat, stirring, until the sugar has completely dissolved, about 5 minutes, then remove the pan from the heat to cool.

3. Slide a butter knife under a corner of the thin white membrane on the bone side of the spareribs to free it from the meat. Using a dry towel for grip, peel off the entire membrane and discard it. Pat the ribs dry with paper towels and season on both sides with the pork rub.

4. When the temperature in the smoker reaches 300°F and the smoke is running clear, add the ribs bone-side down. After 1½ hours, test the ribs for doneness by flipping a rack and pressing the meat between the bones. If the meat pulls away from the bones, it's done. If not, continue smoking until it does, about 30 minutes more.

5. When the ribs are done, gently brush them with the glaze, being careful not to remove the beautiful bark that forms on the exterior of the meat. Cut between the bones and serve with a side of sauce.

MABEL'S PIG EARS

When we decided to put pig ears on the menu at Mabel's, we got tons of jokes that included the phrase "dog treats." But as soon as reluctant diners try them, they immediately see what we love. We brine the ears, then slowly braise them in smoked pork fat before cutting them into strips and flash-frying them. The result is an addictively chewy, smoky, and delicious treat, though I'm pretty sure my dog, Ozzie, wouldn't turn up his nose at them, either! You can strain and refrigerate the pork fat to use again or to make Mabel's Pigtails (page 38).

5 pounds pig ears

2 cups plus ½ teaspoon kosher salt, plus extra for serving

1 cup packed light brown sugar

Pork fat to cover the ears (about 1 gallon)

Cooking oil (optional)

1 cup (2 sticks) unsalted butter, softened

⅔ cup Secret Aardvark Habanero Hot Sauce or your favorite hot sauce

Zest and juice of ½ lime

Oil or lard, for deep-frying

1. Rinse the ears in cold water and check them closely for any hairs, using a blowtorch to singe off any that remain.

2. In a large container, whisk to combine 2 cups of the salt, the brown sugar, and 2 gallons of ice-cold water until the salt and sugar have fully dissolved. Place the ears in the brine, keeping them submerged below the surface with a plate weighed down with a heavy can. Refrigerate overnight.

3. Prepare and preheat your smoker to 225°F.

4. Place the pork fat in a heavy-duty Dutch oven. When the temperature in the smoker reaches 225°F and the smoke is running clear, add the Dutch oven and smoke the fat until it has fully melted and has taken on a smoky flavor, about 1 hour.

5. Preheat the oven to 200°F.

6. Remove the ears from the brine and pat dry with paper towels. Discard the brine. Add the ears to the smoked pork fat, making sure they are completely submerged. If more fat is needed, add cooking oil. Tightly cover the pot with two layers of aluminum foil and cook in the oven until the ears are gelatinous and offer no resistance to a sharp knife, about 10 hours. The ears should be completely limp and lay flat in the pot. Remove from the oven, uncover, and allow to cool enough to handle, about 1 hour. Remove the cooled ears from the fat and refrigerate them until they are completely chilled to ease slicing. Slice the ears into ½-inch-wide strips.

(Recipe continues)

7. In a medium bowl, mix to combine the butter, hot sauce, lime zest, lime juice, and remaining ½ teaspoon salt. When smooth, set aside until needed.

8. In a deep fryer or heavy-bottomed pot set over medium-high heat, heat about 4 inches of oil or lard to 330°F. Fry the ears in batches until golden brown and crisp, using a slotted spoon or frying spider to turn them often, about 5 minutes. When done, remove the ears using the slotted spoon and drain on a paper towel–lined plate. Season with salt and toss in a large bowl with enough of the hot sauce mixture to coat. Serve immediately.

CAREY BRINGLE

Peg Leg Porker

SPECIALTY: Memphis-Style Dry Ribs

"These days, so many of the barbecue places feel like they have to be everything to everybody," says Carey Bringle, owner of Nashville-based Peg Leg Porker. "We chose to be different when we opened and just serve what was traditionally known as real Tennessee barbecue, and that's pork ribs, butts, and chicken."

Bringle converted twenty-five years on the competitive barbecue circuit, namely Memphis in May, into his popular brick-and-mortar restaurant, Peg Leg Porker. A longtime fan of true Memphis-style ribs, made famous by that city's seventy-year-old Rendezvous barbecue restaurant, Bringle decided to introduce his Nashville customers to the concept of a sauceless rib.

"We had to educate the consumer a little bit about what they are and how they're prepared," he says. "What we do in Nashville is a style very similar to the way the Rendezvous does it, but we do it a little bit different."

The key difference is the cooking method, he explains. The Rendezvous opts for "hot and fast," cooking their racks of ribs over hot charcoal for a relatively shorter time. Bringle seasons his baby back ribs with salt and smokes them over native hickory wood for anywhere between three and four hours. Just like the folks at the Rendezvous, he seasons the ribs with his proprietary sixteen-ingredient spice blend right before they hit the plate.

"This is not really a rub—it is a barbecue seasoning that is meant to replace barbecue sauce," he explains. "It's meant to be added after the product is cooked, so what you get is the full flavor of the pork and the full flavor of the spices without cooking out any of that brightness."

When Bringle first opened the shop, he offered his guests a choice between wet and dry ribs. He since has yanked the sauce-slathered ribs off the menu and hasn't looked back.

"We finally took the wet ribs off because the dry ribs are what we're best at," he says. "We're proud of our ribs, and if you want the true Peg Leg Porker experience, then this is what you need to order. Sure, some folks will dip them in sauce, but a lot of people are die-hard and want their ribs without sauce. That dry seasoning makes it so you don't even need it."

MABEL'S PIGTAILS

Just like with our pig ears, pigtails taste so much better than they sound—especially when they're slowly braised in lard, deep-fried, and tossed in a buttery hot sauce. Thanks to a delicious combination of skin, meat, and fat, they are like the pig version of the chicken wing. You can strain and refrigerate the pork fat to use again or to make Mabel's Pig Ears (page 34).

5 pounds skin-on pigtails

2 cups plus ½ teaspoon kosher salt, plus extra for serving

1 cup packed light brown sugar

Pork fat to cover the tails (about 1 gallon)

Cooking oil (optional)

1 cup (2 sticks) unsalted butter, softened

⅔ cup Secret Aardvark Habanero Hot Sauce or your favorite hot sauce

Zest and juice of ½ lime

Oil or lard, for deep-frying

1. If your pigtails arrive whole, cut off and discard the last 2 inches from the skinny end of the tail. Cut the remaining tail pieces into 4-inch segments. Trim off and discard any large pieces of fat.

2. In a large container, whisk 2 cups of the salt, the brown sugar, and 2 gallons of ice-cold water until dissolved. Submerge the tails in the brine, keeping them below the surface with a plate weighed down with a heavy can. Refrigerate overnight.

3. Preheat the oven to 200°F.

4. Drain the tails (discard the brine) and pat dry with paper towels. Put the tails in a large Dutch oven. In a separate large saucepan, warm the pork fat over medium heat until it is liquefied. Carefully pour the melted fat over the tails, making sure they are completely submerged. If more fat is needed, add cooking oil. Tightly cover the pot with two layers of aluminum foil and cook in the oven until the tails are gelatinous and offer no resistance to a sharp knife, about 10 hours. Remove the pot from the oven, uncover, and allow to cool, about 1 hour. When the tails are cool enough to handle, remove them from the fat.

5. In a medium bowl, mix the butter, hot sauce, lime zest, lime juice, and remaining ½ teaspoon salt until smooth. Set aside.

6. In a deep fryer or heavy-bottomed pot set over medium-high heat, heat about 4 inches of oil or lard to 330°F. Fry the tails in batches, uncovered, until golden brown and crisp, using a slotted spoon or frying spider to turn them often, about 5 minutes. When done, remove the tails using a slotted spoon and drain on a paper towel–lined plate. Season with salt and toss in a large bowl with enough hot sauce to coat. Serve immediately.

PATRICK MARTIN
Martin's Bar-B-Que Joint

SPECIALTY: West Tennessee–Style Whole-Hog BBQ

"If you define the five major barbecue regions as Memphis, Eastern North Carolina, Western North Carolina, Texas, and Kansas City, you're skipping over a lot of very influential and important subregions that never get addressed," explains Patrick Martin of Martin's Bar-B-Que Joint. "The barbecue I learned to cook is one hundred miles from Memphis, but it is not Memphis barbecue. My style is West Tennessee, and in West Tennessee we do whole hog, period, and that's it."

With multiple locations in and around Nashville, West Virginia, and Kentucky, Martin's Bar-B-Que Joint was built on that West Tennessee tradition of whole-hog barbecue. While there are similarities with Carolina-style whole-hog barbecue, Martin is quick to mention that the styles are not one and the same. Over there, they cook smaller hogs at slightly higher temperatures. And when the pork is done, they chop it up, fold in their preferred accent flavors, and serve.

In West Tennessee, they smoke meaty 200-pound hogs at 200°F for roughly 24 hours over live coals. While it sounds pretty straightforward in principle, the technique is challenging as heck in practice, says Martin.

"You have three very distinct primals that are all different thicknesses, different fat contents, and different collagen levels in the muscle fibers," he explains. "Hams take longer than the shoulders or belly. And to get all three of them done without undercooking or overcooking one of them is where the skill comes in. That's why cooking whole hog is so hard, and why there's not a lot of people who do it."

Given its impressive girth, Tennessee whole hog is not prepared in a traditional offset smoker. It is cooked on a pit, typically assembled out of common cinder blocks picked up at the local hardware store. The pit is fueled by well-seasoned hickory, which is added by the shovelful when good and glowing.

When the meat is ready to serve, it is not chopped up and mixed together; it is pulled by hand and kept separate for the customers who know exactly what parts they want.

"People in West Tennessee are very particular about what muscle they want," Martin says. "Some will ask for a sandwich of cheek meat and belly meat, but they don't want ham or shoulder. And when we make a sandwich, it is always served with slaw. That is absolutely nonnegotiable. We like to say, 'That's the way God meant for you to have a barbecue sandwich.'"

MABEL'S CRACKLINGS

This is an adaptation of a cracklings recipe that I learned from the great chef Paul Kahan, who shared his technique with me one night at the Publican in Chicago. We have been serving a version of them at Lola and Mabel's ever since. Unlike traditional cracklings, which often have chewy bits of meat and fat still attached to the skin, these are more like light and airy pork rinds. We dust them fresh out of the fryer with salt and malt vinegar powder (available online), which adds a nice tang without making them soggy like regular vinegar. We serve them with Lawson's French Onion Dip, a creamy dip that most Clevelanders grew up with. If you can't get your hands on the original, any sour cream–based French onion dip will do.

1 pound pork skin, cut into 4 equal pieces

¼ cup kosher salt

½ cup malt vinegar powder

Oil or lard, for deep-frying

1 cup Lawson's French Onion Dip or other sour cream–based onion dip

1. In a large saucepan, bring 4 quarts of water to a simmer over medium heat. Add the pork skins and cook until they are soft and somewhat gelatinous, about 1 hour. Drain the skins (discard the liquid) and arrange them in a single layer on a parchment paper–lined baking sheet. Refrigerate the skins for 15 minutes so they will be easier to handle.

2. Put one of the skins on a cutting board skin-side down. With a very sharp knife, remove as much of the meat and fat as possible and discard it, being careful not to slice into the skin. This makes the dried skins light and crispy. Repeat with the remaining pieces.

3. Preheat the oven to 300°F. Line a baking sheet with parchment paper.

4. Arrange the skins on the prepared baking sheet and cook in the oven for 1½ hours. Flip the skins and cook until the skins are completely dry and brittle, about 1½ hours. Remove from the oven and let cool. When cool enough to handle, scrape off any lingering bits of fat and meat with the back of a knife. At this point, the cracklings can be stored in an airtight container in the refrigerator for up to 3 weeks.

5. Mix together the salt and malt vinegar powder in a small bowl.

6. In a deep fryer or heavy-bottomed pot set over medium-high heat, heat about 4 inches of oil or lard to 350°F. Break the cracklings into 1-inch pieces. Fry in batches until crisp and puffy, using the slotted spoon or a frying spider to turn them often, about 45 seconds. When done, remove the skins using the slotted spoon and drain on a paper towel–lined plate. Season with the salt–vinegar powder mixture. Serve immediately with Lawson's French Onion Dip on the side.

SMOKED PORK BUTT

One of the best cuts for beginning smokers, the pork shoulder is almost foolproof thanks to thick seams of lubricating fat, which prevent the meat from drying out during the long cook time. While whole pork shoulders can clock in at well over ten pounds, the smaller Boston butt is more manageable in size. Theories as to why it's called the butt, despite the fact that it comes from the shoulder, range from the way hogs butt up to each other shoulder to shoulder to the fact that the cuts used to be packed into barrels (once called butts) for shipping. I offer two different methods based on whether you plan to slice and serve the roast or shred it into classic pulled pork. At 185°F, the meat is tender, but still holds together for slicing. At 203°F, the pork breaks down into meat that is easily shredded by hand.

1 (6- to 8-pound) bone-in pork butt, trimmed of loose-hanging fat

2 tablespoons yellow mustard

1 cup Pork Rub (page 234)

1. Prepare and preheat your smoker to 225°F.

2. Pat the pork dry with paper towels and coat the entire exterior with the mustard. Season on all sides with the pork rub.

3. When the temperature in the smoker reaches 225°F and the smoke is running clear, add the pork and cook until the meat reaches an internal temperature of 185°F for slicing, or 203°F for pulling, anywhere from 12 to 14 hours. For the best results, use a probe thermometer to continually monitor the meat's temperature.

4. Slice or pull the pork according to your preference and serve.

SAMUEL JONES
Skylight Inn BBQ

SPECIALTY: Eastern North Carolina–Style Whole-Hog BBQ

"It all boils down to what piece of dirt you're standing on as to what somebody calls barbecue," Sam Jones says. "Here at the Skylight, whole hog has always been what we do."

Not much has changed since Sam's granddad Pete Jones opened the modest barbecue restaurant Skylight Inn on the site of the original family farm in Ayden, North Carolina. There, "barbecue" still means whole hogs cooked in a pit over real wood. The meat is chopped and served as a sandwich or in a paper boat topped with a thin slice of cornbread and a side of sweet coleslaw.

The way Jones tells it, his neck of Eastern North Carolina used to be flush with whole-hog barbecue restaurants, but these days he can count that number on one hand.

"People don't do it anymore," he reports. "Unfortunately, as the years passed, whole-hog places have fallen by the wayside because either there was not a generation to succeed the previous one or the generation that did succeed them saw fit to change it."

At Skylight—and now also Sam Jones BBQ outside Greenville, North Carolina—they cook 175- to 190-pound hogs that are butter-flied and laid meat-side down in rustic block pits. The skin is salted and the hogs cook low and slow over oak wood coals for between 16 and 18 hours. The optimal pit temperature is 250°F, not that there are any thermometers lying around. About 5 or 6 hours into the cook, the pig is flipped skin-side down, a move that would likely spark outrage in dearly departed Pete, Jones admits.

"Being able to travel and work with some smart minds in food, I always try and stay a constant student," Jones says. "What I've learned is that some of the stuff my granddad did didn't make a bit of damn sense. Just because something's been done one way for fifty years doesn't mean it was done right."

Forever, the pitmasters at Skylight would wait until the next morning to flip the pigs, Jones explains. But given the advanced state of tenderness at that final hour, some pigs would fall to pieces or, at the very least, you'd lose some meat to the floor of the pit.

"What I learned is that it didn't make a damn bit of difference," Jones reports. "I personally think that we're selling a better product than we ever had because we've got it figured out."

But most things at Skylight will never change. Behind the counter, a half hog is chopped at a time, ensuring that diners will get a flavorful mix of meat from the shoulder, ham, belly, and loin. The golden brown skin is also chopped and folded into the meat, giving you a little bit of delicious crunch in every bite. The chopped, blended meat is dressed— not sauced—simply with vinegar, black pepper, and hot sauce.

While he's not one to disparage other barbecue cooks, Jones does think that people who eat only pulled pork shoulder are missing out on pork barbecue's true flavor potential.

"It's as different as eating bacon and eating a hamburger," he explains. "The idea behind whole-hog barbecue is to be able to blend together all of the meat. You don't get that cooking shoulders; you're missing the best parts of the hog, which is the bacon and the jowl."

SMOKED CROWN ROAST
of Pork

In many cultures, the pig has been a symbol of good luck for ages. As the superstition goes, if you eat pork on New Year's Day, you are guaranteed to have a good and prosperous New Year. If regular pork is good luck, this smoked crown roast is bound to bring great luck for many years to come, because it is so impressive and delicious.

2 tablespoons kosher salt

1 tablespoon freshly ground black pepper

2 tablespoons caraway seeds

1½ teaspoons celery seeds

1 (10- to 12-pound) crown roast of pork

1. Prepare and preheat your smoker to 325°F.

2. In a small bowl, mix to combine the salt, pepper, caraway seeds, and celery seeds. Pat the roast dry with paper towels and season on all sides with the spice mixture.

3. When the temperature in the smoker reaches 325°F and the smoke is running clear, add the meat. Cook until the pork reaches an internal temperature of 150°F, about 2½ hours. For the best results, use a probe thermometer to continually monitor the meat's temperature.

4. Transfer the pork to a cutting board and let rest for 30 minutes. Slice between the bones and serve.

GRILLED PORK TENDERLOIN
with Mostarda

This is a great recipe for people who are just getting their grill game going. Not only is it easy as pie to master, but the combination of grilled pork and mostarda is a showstopper. Mostarda is a sweet-and-savory condiment made with fruit, herbs, and spices that goes great not only with grilled meats but also rich cheeses. Mostarda can be stored for months in the refrigerator, so go ahead and make a big batch so you always have some on hand when you fire up the grill.

Juice of 1 lime

1 tablespoon Dijon mustard

1 tablespoon soy sauce

2 (1-pound) pork tenderloins, trimmed of silver skin

1 tablespoon ground toasted coriander seeds

1 tablespoon kosher salt

Mostarda (recipe follows)

1. Prepare and preheat your lump charcoal grill to create two heat zones: high and medium.

2. In a small bowl, mix to combine the lime juice, mustard, and soy sauce. Pat the tenderloin dry with paper towels and apply this mixture to the exterior of the pork. Season the meat with the coriander and salt.

3. Sear the pork over the hot side of the grill until the exterior forms a nice crust, about 4 minutes per side. Move the pork to the medium side of the grill, cover the grill, and cook until the pork reaches an internal temperature of 140°F.

4. Transfer the pork to a cutting board, tent it loosely with aluminum foil, and let rest for 15 to 20 minutes. Thinly slice the pork crosswise into ¼-inch-thick pieces. Serve with mostarda on top and more on the side for those who want it.

(Recipe continues)

Mostarda

1½ teaspoons coriander seeds

1½ teaspoons mustard seeds

1 medium shallot, thinly sliced

1 Granny Smith apple, peeled, cored, and cut into medium dice

1 peach, peeled, pitted, and cut into medium dice

1 star anise pod

1 tablespoon fresh thyme leaves

1 cup sugar

1½ cups cider vinegar

Kosher salt and freshly ground black pepper

2 tablespoons chopped crystallized ginger

In a medium saucepan, toast the coriander and mustard seeds over medium-high heat for 1 minute. Add the shallot, apple, peach, star anise, thyme, sugar, and vinegar and bring to a boil. Reduce the heat to low and simmer until the fruit softens and the liquid reduces and thickens, about 20 minutes.

Remove from the heat and season with salt and pepper. Stir in the ginger and set aside to cool. Use immediately or store in the refrigerator in an airtight container for up to 2 weeks.

MIKE & AMY MILLS
17th Street Barbecue

SPECIALTY: Southern Illinois–Style Pork Steak

"My father's first memory was waking up to the smell of barbecue smoke," Amy Mills relates about her father, Mike, who is simply referred to as "the Legend" by his pitmaster peers, thanks to a matchless track record at Memphis in May, where the World Championship Barbecue Contest is a highlight of the month-long festival. "He later fulfilled his father's dream of bottling the family sauce and opening a barbecue restaurant."

That restaurant, 17th Street Barbecue in sleepy Murphysboro, Illinois, sits almost equidistant from three robust barbecue regions, each of which influenced certain aspects of the Southern Illinois barbecue scene, says Amy. "We're two hours south of St. Louis and three hours from both Nashville and Memphis. But we have a very rich barbecue heritage and have over these many years developed our own barbecue culture that is unique to Southern Illinois."

Walk into 17th Street Barbecue and order the ribs, and you'll likely be reminded of Memphis, thanks to the meaty baby backs that are smoked low and slow and served, not slathered with sauce, but dry rubbed with a proprietary spice blend known as Magic Dust that is designed to accentuate, not conceal, the flavor of the pork.

"You should taste four things in your mouth when you're eating barbecue," Amy says. "You should taste a little smoke, you should taste the seasoning and the sauce, and you should taste the meat itself. We are surrounded by apple orchards here, and fruit wood is milder and sweeter, which allows the flavor of the meat to shine through."

As popular as those Memphis-style dry ribs are, the St. Louis–style pork steaks have been cultivating a fan base all their own for decades. This uniquely Midwestern preparation might have started in the backyards of local barbecue wizards, but it has long since expanded outside the region—because they are too good not to.

For the famous pork steaks, the butt end of the pork shoulder is sliced on a band saw into meaty one-pound steaks. Those steaks are seasoned with Magic Dust, popped into the smoker, and allowed to cook for about two hours at a low 210°F. To finish, they are sauced and tossed on a hot grill to sear and caramelize both sides.

"Barbecue is a culture, not a concept—and the cream will always rise to the top," Amy says.

GRILLED PORK CHOPS

I remember when we first started serving pork chops at Lola twenty years ago. We've always worked hard to source the best meat that money can buy, and we were thrilled to get our hands on some amazing acorn-fed Red Wattle pork, a heritage breed. Because the flavor of the pork is so rich and intense, we were able to season it pretty aggressively. Soon after the first order went out, the customer sent it right back. I went out to the table to ask what was wrong and the gentleman said the chops tasted "too porky"! While I'm never happy when a customer isn't completely satisfied, I was thrilled we had finally found pork that actually tasted like pork—the kind of flavor my grandfather would recognize. I sent the customer some chicken and Lola continues to serve "porky" pork to this day.

1 tablespoon coriander seeds, cracked

1 tablespoon ground chipotle chile powder

1 tablespoon kosher salt

½ tablespoon ground cumin

½ tablespoon smoked paprika

¾ teaspoon mustard powder

6 (10- to 12-ounce) double-cut pork chops

3 tablespoons olive oil

1. Prepare and preheat your lump charcoal grill to create two heat zones: high and low.

2. In a small bowl, mix to combine the coriander, chipotle, salt, cumin, paprika, and mustard powder. Pat the chops dry with paper towels and season both sides with the spice mixture. Rub the exterior of the seasoned chops with the olive oil.

3. Sear the chops over the hot side of the grill until the exterior forms a nice crust, about 4 minutes per side. Move the pork to the low-heat side of the grill, cover the grill, and cook until the pork reaches an internal temperature of 140°F, about 12 minutes. Transfer the pork to a cutting board, let it rest for 5 to 10 minutes, and then serve.

HOUSE BACON

At Lola, we were curing and smoking our own bacon long before it was popular to do so. We learned early on that we could make a better-tasting product than most of the stuff on the market. This is the recipe we've relied on for two decades at our restaurants! It makes a good amount, which is great since it freezes beautifully for a few months.

3 tablespoons kosher salt

1½ tablespoons packed light brown sugar

1 teaspoon pink curing salt (see note)

6 pounds uncured pork belly

Pink Curing Salt

Pink curing salt—sometimes called pink salt, curing salt, or Prague Powder—is a carefully blended mixture of salt, sodium nitrite, and/or sodium nitrate used to preserve meats and prevent botulism. Not to be confused with Himalayan pink salt, pink curing salt should not be used or consumed like regular salt, which is why it is tinted pink to visually differentiate it.

1. In a small bowl, mix to combine the kosher salt, sugar, and curing salt. Pat the pork dry with paper towels and thoroughly coat the exterior with the seasoning mixture, using all of it.

2. Line a baking sheet large enough to hold the pork with parchment paper. Place the pork on the baking sheet, cover it with another piece of parchment paper, place a second baking sheet on top, and weigh it all down with a heavy pan or a heavy can (or cans). Cure in the refrigerator for 7 days.

3. After 7 days, discard the juices that have collected in the baking sheet and rinse the pork under cold water. Place the belly on a flat roasting rack positioned on a baking sheet and refrigerate, uncovered, overnight to dry the exterior.

4. Prepare and preheat your smoker to 250°F. When the temperature reaches 250°F and the smoke is running clear, remove the pork from the roasting rack and add it to the smoker. Cook until the meat reaches an internal temperature of 165°F, about 3½ hours. For the best results, use a probe thermometer to continually monitor the meat's temperature.

5. Remove the pork from the smoker and refrigerate, uncovered, for several hours or up to overnight. Slice to desired thickness and use immediately or wrap in two layers of plastic wrap and store in the refrigerator for up to 1 week or in the freezer for up to 2 months.

RODNEY SCOTT

Scott's Bar-B-Que

SPECIALTY: Eastern South Carolina–Style Whole-Hog BBQ

Rodney Scott was just eleven years old when he started cooking at the family restaurant. And since that family restaurant happened to be a barbecue joint in Hemingway, South Carolina, that meant he was cooking whole hogs.

"Down our way, you didn't see a lot of shoulders; it was mostly the whole hog," Rodney says. "That was because a lot of folks in the area had farms and they would do big celebrations at the end of the harvest. Whole hog was the most inexpensive way to do that because you can feed over a hundred people with it."

As the family farms began to dry up, shops like Scott's Bar-B-Que, which was opened by Rodney's parents, Ella and Roosevelt Scott, kept that rich and delicious whole-hog barbecue tradition alive. That restaurant opened up in 1972 and still attracts hungry barbecue pilgrims to this day.

"If you really think about it, who wants to give half a day away getting ready to eat?" Rodney says of the 12 hours it takes to cook a pig.

But that half day is nothing compared to the time it takes to cut down trees (oak, hickory, pecan), saw them into logs, and split those logs into manageable pieces of wood, all of which Rodney and his family have always done themselves. All that wood makes its way through tall burn barrels that turn timber into glowing-hot embers, which are moved, shovel by shovel, to the huge pits, where they are strategically scattered beneath butterflied whole hogs.

"They go on fresh, belly-side down," Rodney says of the 150-pound hogs. "We cook them for twelve hours at 220° to 250°F and flip them at the end to crisp up the skin. That's when we season and mop them."

When the hog is done cooking, it is deboned and all the juicy, slow-cooked meat is pulled, sauced, and tossed. Unlike the West Tennessee–style whole hog that Patrick Martin (see page 39) does, which keeps the various cuts of pork separate after cooking, the Scotts mix everything together.

"I personally like to mix the hams, shoulders, loins, and bellies all up together because you get that stiffness of the loin, that tenderness of the belly, and in between with the shoulder," he explains. "The juices from the belly lay across the loin and keep it moist while it's cooking. This way you never get an extremely dry piece of pork."

The meat is dressed with a thin vinegar-and-pepper sauce that is very characteristic of Eastern South Carolina. Unlike the barbecue sauces found elsewhere in the Carolinas, this one does not contain any mustard. Most people enjoy that tender, savory, and succulent meat by the pound or in a sandwich. True fans know to add a few pieces of that golden crackling skin to their orders.

Each week, the Hemingway spot goes through more than twenty-five hogs, adding proof to Rodney's claim that there is no better barbecue than Carolina-style whole-hog barbecue.

"It's been my experience that when you cook the whole hog together, you can taste the difference," he says. "You get a more incorporated flavor of everything. The juices out the backbones connect with the juices in the hambones and all of the stuff is being cooked together at the same time and the flavors penetrate all the way through."

MABEL'S HUNGARIAN
Smoked Kielbasa

When it came time to select the kielbasa that would be served at Mabel's, I didn't have to think about it for long. My favorite smoked sausage comes from J & J Czuchraj Meats, which has been a fixture of the West Side Market for more than sixty years, and this recipe comes straight from them. At J & J, they go many steps above the average sausage maker when crafting their Hungarian kielbasa, which is precisely why I love them. They use all-natural, antibiotic-free pork shoulder and beef cheek meat, hand-cut garlic (not powder), and natural casings (not synthetic), and they smoke them over real hickory wood in a hundred-year-old smoker. At Mabel's we offer both the classic and the hot with cheese varieties. (To experience J & J Czuchraj Meats' magic without having to make your own sausage, call the meat market at 216-696-7083.)

7 pounds medium-ground boneless pork shoulder

3 pounds medium-ground boneless beef cheek

½ ounce granulated onion

1 ounce minced garlic cloves

2 ounces kosher salt

½ ounce freshly ground black pepper

1 teaspoon ground nutmeg

½ ounce pink curing salt (see Note, page 56)

1 pound pork casings, rinsed and soaked in cold water until needed

1. In a very large bowl, combine the pork, beef, onion, garlic, salt, spices, and 1 cup cold water. Mix thoroughly to combine. Refrigerate until ready to use.

2. Following the instructions for your sausage machine, stuff the filling into the pork casings, twist or tie them into 6- to 8-inch links, and refrigerate for at least 6 hours to allow them to cure.

3. Prepare and preheat your smoker to 200°F.

4. When the temperature in the smoker reaches 200°F and the smoke is running clear, add the sausage and cook until it reaches an internal temperature of 165°F, about 3 hours. For the best results, use a probe thermometer to continually monitor the meat's temperature.

5. Remove the sausages from the smoker and chill them in cold water for 5 minutes to prevent wrinkling. To prepare, grill, boil, or sauté the kielbasa until hot and serve. Or use in This Is Cleveland (page 66).

Since I was a child, the West Side Market has continued to spark inspiration for me on what and how to cook. This 105-year-old public market is a meat (and seafood, and cheese, and bread) lover's paradise!

THIS IS CLEVELAND

One of the things I miss most about not being in Cleveland for all the Browns football games is having the gang over for our weekly "tailgate" parties. Sure, we watch football, but since it's the Browns, we mostly eat, laugh, and argue our way through one painful season after another. This smoky, tart, and savory dish is like a tailgate party on a plate because it contains the kinds of foods you'd see at every home game: beer-braised pork, kielbasa, and kraut. I was stuck in New York for one Thursday-night game and invited some Giants-loving chefs and football buddies over to watch the game. This is the dish I made for them, and they were so busy gobbling it all up that they didn't even have time to make fun of the Browns' performance!

Braised Pork

2 tablespoons unsalted butter

1 medium onion, cut into medium dice

1 head white cabbage, cut into medium dice

Kosher salt

4 cups apple cider

1 cup sauerkraut

1 (12-ounce) IPA beer

1 tablespoon crushed red pepper flakes

1 tablespoon ground coriander

1 smoked ham hock

½ rack (about 1 pound) smoked bone-in pork loin (can substitute good-quality smoked ham)

2 pounds kielbasa

Dumpling Dough

3 large eggs

¾ cup unsweetened applesauce

1½ teaspoons kosher salt

2 cups all-purpose flour

To Serve

1 bunch fresh flat-leaf parsley, coarsely chopped

¼ cup hot mustard

Kosher salt and freshly ground black pepper

(Recipe continues)

1. Make the braised pork: In a Dutch oven, melt the butter over medium-high heat. When the butter has melted, add the onion and cabbage and season with salt. Cook, stirring occasionally, until the vegetables have softened, about 6 minutes.

2. Meanwhile, in a blender or food processer, combine the cider and sauerkraut and blend or purée until smooth. When the onions and cabbage are soft, add the sauerkraut mixture to the saucepan, along with the beer, red pepper flakes, coriander, ham hock, smoked pork loin, and sausage. Bring to a simmer, cover, and cook until the meat is tender and the flavors have permeated throughout, about 1½ hours.

3. Meanwhile, make the dumpling dough: In a large bowl, whisk to combine the eggs and applesauce. Add the salt and flour and mix to combine. Set aside until ready to use.

4. When the meat is cooked through, transfer the ham hock, pork, and sausage to a cutting board. Place the dumpling dough on a lightly dampened cutting board and cut the dough into 1-inch pieces. Drop the dumplings directly into the hot braising liquid. Cook the dumplings until they begin to float. Slice the meat and return it to the pot.

5. Remove the pot from the heat, stir in the parsley and mustard, season with salt and freshly ground black pepper, and serve.

If there is a dish that represents my childhood, it's this one. This Is Cleveland can just as easily be called This Is Me, because it combines so many of my favorite food memories.

BEEF

MABEL'S PASTRAMI

For me, pastrami is the great-granddaddy of smoked meats. To make it, beef brisket is corned—or cured—before going into the smoker, resulting in a luscious product that is salty, smoky, and heavily spiced. When buying brisket, you have options: there is the fattier point half, the leaner flat half, or the whole blessed brisket. While this recipe is great for the leaner flat because it keeps it moist and delicious, we use whole briskets because we like offering guests a choice of cuts. There are plenty of great pastramis in the world, but to me, none is better than what's made and served at Katz's Deli on the Lower East Side of Manhattan. If you are going to strive for anything, this is the place to emulate. As the old woman famously said while seated in Katz's Deli in *When Harry Met Sally*: "I'll have what she's having."

1 (12- to 15-pound) brisket

Brine

⅓ cup pink curing salt (see Note, page 56)

½ cup packed light brown sugar

2 tablespoons coriander seeds

2 tablespoons coarsely ground black pepper

6 garlic cloves, crushed

3 quarts of ice

Rub

½ cup freshly ground black pepper

½ cup coriander seeds, cracked

¼ cup yellow mustard seeds, cracked

¼ cup kosher salt

2 tablespoons crushed red pepper flakes

Cleveland BBQ Sauce (page 220), for serving (optional)

(Recipe continues)

1. Prepare the brisket by trimming the fat cap to create a fatty side and a lean side. Remove all but about ½ inch of fat on the "flat," or thinner half, of the brisket, and about 1 inch on the "point," or thicker side. Turn the brisket over and remove any sinew or silver skin from the meat side of the brisket. You should expect to trim and discard up to 2 pounds of fat and silver skin on a large brisket.

2. Make the brine: In a large stockpot, combine 2 quarts (8 cups) water, the curing salt, brown sugar, coriander, black pepper, and garlic. Bring the mixture to a gentle boil over high heat, occasionally stirring to dissolve the salt and sugar. Remove the pot from the heat, add the ice, and allow the brine to cool completely. Lower the brisket into the brine, keeping it submerged below the surface with a plate weighed down with a heavy can. Refrigerate for 4 days.

3. Prepare and preheat your smoker to 225°F.

4. Make the rub: In a medium bowl, mix to combine the black pepper, coriander, mustard seeds, salt, and red pepper flakes.

5. Remove the brisket from the brine, discard the brine, and pat the brisket dry with paper towels. Liberally season it on all sides with the rub. When the temperature in the smoker reaches 225°F and the smoke is running clear, add the brisket, fat-side up. Cook the brisket until it reaches an internal temperature of 195°F, between 12 and 15 hours. For the best results, use a probe thermometer to continually monitor the meat's temperature.

6. To serve, slice the flat portion of the brisket against the grain into ¼-inch pieces (about the same thickness as a pencil) until you reach the thick ribbon of fat that separates it from the point. Turn the point portion of the brisket 90 degrees so that you can continue slicing the meat against the grain. Serve immediately or hold according to the instructions on page 23. I like my brisket "naked," but you can drizzle on some sauce, if you like.

MABEL'S GIANT BEEF RIBS

The first time I tasted real-deal smoked beef ribs was at the New York City–based Daisy May's BBQ, chef Adam Perry Lang's first restaurant. I can just hear all my Texas-based barbecue snobs now: *Manhattan? Are you kidding me?* Let me assure you that few human beings on the planet know as much about meat and barbecue as Perry Lang, and his mind-blowing version of beef ribs forever changed how I felt about barbecue. The version of giant beef ribs that we serve at Mabel's is inspired by that experience. To make them "Cleveland style," we rub them liberally with our pastrami spices in honor of our eastern European heritage.

1 (3-bone) rack beef plate ribs (about 5 pounds)

1 cup Beef Rib Rub (page 234)

1. Prepare and preheat your smoker to 225°F.

2. Pat the ribs dry with paper towels and season on all sides with the beef rib rub.

3. When the temperature in the smoker reaches 225°F and the smoke is running clear, add the beef ribs, meat-side up. Cook until the beef ribs reach an internal temperature of 200°F, about 7 hours. For the best results, use a probe thermometer to continually monitor the meat's temperature.

4. Slice the meat between the bones and serve immediately, or hold according to the instructions on page 23.

MABEL'S BRISKET

If you agree that Central Texas is home to the best barbecue in the world, then you are probably as passionate about beef brisket as I am. But nobody is as passionate about brisket as the folks from Black's BBQ in Lockhart, a city just outside of Austin that is often called the Barbecue Capital of Texas. When it comes to barbecue, brisket is the hardest cut of meat to master because each piece contains two very different types of meat: the fattier point and the leaner flat. The pitmaster must maintain just the right amount of heat, smoke, and humidity for hours and hours to achieve a tender point and moist flat. Black's nails it every single time. So do the folks at Franklin and La Barbecue, both in Austin. At Mabel's, we might use local fruit woods in place of native Texas post oak, but our barbecue style originates in smoke-filled Central Texas.

1 (12- to 15-pound) brisket

1 recipe Cleveland BBQ Sauce (page 220)

1 cup Basic Rub (page 234)

1. Prepare the brisket by trimming the fat cap to create a fatty side and a lean side. Remove all but about ½ inch of fat on the "flat," or thinner half, of the brisket, and about 1 inch on the "point," or thicker side. Turn the brisket over and remove any sinew or silver skin from the meat side of the brisket. You should expect to trim and discard up to 2 pounds of fat and silver skin on a large brisket.

2. Prepare and preheat your smoker to 225°F.

3. Pat the brisket dry with paper towels and coat the entire exterior with the barbecue sauce. Season liberally on all sides with the basic rub.

4. When the temperature in the smoker reaches 225°F and the smoke is running clear, add the brisket, fat-side up. Cook until the meat reaches an internal temperature of 195°F, between 12 and 15 hours. For the best results, use a probe thermometer to continually monitor the meat's temperature.

5. To serve, slice the flat portion of the brisket against the grain until you reach the thick ribbon of fat that separates it from the point. Turn the point portion of the brisket 90 degrees so that you can continue slicing the meat against the grain. Serve immediately or hold according to the instructions on page 23. Save any trimmings to use in Brisket Melts (page 86) or Brisket Baked Lima Beans (page 195).

KENT BLACK
Black's BBQ

SPECIALTY: Central Texas–Style Beef Brisket

Central Texas is cattle country, so it makes sense that Central Texas–style barbecue is all about beef, especially beef brisket. And nobody does it better than Black's BBQ in Lockhart, which cuts meat on butcher blocks that are older than most of Austin's new-wave joints.

"Lockhart is on the Chisholm Trail, where cowboys would drive the cattle herds from the ranches of South Texas right up through Austin, Fort Worth, and up to the railheads of Kansas," explains Kent Black, third-generation owner. "We've always had a cattle culture here in Lockhart."

Spend any amount of time with Kent and he'll likely share the story about how at the height of the Great Depression, his granddad parlayed one hundred head of cattle into his own meat market, which is how all barbecue restaurants got their start back in the day.

"Back in the 1930s, there was very little refrigeration for meat markets, other than sixty-pound blocks of ice," Black recounts. "Fresh meat would last only a couple days and then you either made it into sausage or smoked it, which would buy you another three or four days of shelf life."

Since 1932, Black's has been offering a master class in beef brisket, which is cooked low and slow in ancient smokers fueled entirely by local post oak.

"Post oak is very plentiful around Lockhart, and it's what my grandfather started with when he opened," says Black. "We continue to use it because you can cook for as long as ten to fourteen hours and it won't give you that bitter taste you can get from hickory or mesquite. We think that makes a big difference in the flavor of the barbecue."

To prepare, the briskets are hand-trimmed, seasoned with a straightforward dry rub, and cooked for hours in lengthy offset smokers. The meat is always sliced to order—from the leaner flat or the fattier point—and served on a butcher paper–lined tray with sliced white bread, dill pickles, and raw onions. Oh, and as for the barbecue sauce, that will be on the side, where it belongs.

"In Texas, you're always judged by how good your brisket is without sauce," Black says. "We don't cook with sauce, and we encourage our customers to taste it without sauce. A lot of people would ask my father what he put on the briskets to make them taste so good. His answer was always 'It's not what we put on it that makes it so good, it's what we *don't* put on it.'"

With brisket and other large-format barbecue items, generous amounts of seasonings enhance both the flavor and the texture of the meat.

As I like to tell my cooks: "Season from on high and don't be shy!"

BRISKET MELTS

Whenever I smoke brisket, I always set aside some of the best pieces and parts to make these killer sandwiches. They are essentially patty melts that swap out the burgers for luscious, mouth-watering beef brisket. Loaded with sweet caramelized onions, melty Swiss cheese, and creamy Russian dressing, these are definitely multi-napkin sandwiches!

1 tablespoon olive oil

1 yellow onion, halved and thinly sliced

Kosher salt

2 pounds chopped smoked brisket

8 slices Swiss cheese

2 tablespoons unsalted butter, softened

8 slices rye bread

Russian Dressing (recipe follows)

4 kosher dill pickles, for serving

1. Preheat the oven to 300°F.

2. In a large skillet, heat the olive oil over medium heat. Add the onion and a pinch of salt. Cook, stirring occasionally, until the onion is soft and well caramelized, about 5 minutes. Reduce the heat to low to keep warm while you prepare the sandwiches.

3. On a parchment paper–lined baking sheet, divide the brisket into four sandwich-size piles, top each pile with two slices of cheese, and place in the oven to warm and melt.

4. Meanwhile, set a large skillet or griddle over medium heat. Butter one side of each piece of bread and place it butter-side down on the skillet. Toast until golden brown, about 1 minute. You might have to toast the bread in batches.

5. When the cheese has melted and the brisket is warm, assemble the sandwiches by spreading Russian dressing on four slices of toast and topping with the onions, brisket with cheese, and finally a second slice of bread, toasted-side up.

6. Serve with a giant kosher dill pickle.

(Recipe continues)

Russian Dressing

½ cup mayonnaise

3 tablespoons ketchup

1 tablespoon finely
chopped onion

1 tablespoon finely
chopped dill pickle, plus
1 tablespoon pickle juice
from the jar

1 tablespoon prepared
horseradish (optional)

1 teaspoon hot sauce

1 teaspoon
Worcestershire sauce

½ teaspoon sweet
paprika

Kosher salt and freshly
ground black pepper

In a medium bowl, whisk to combine the
mayonnaise, ketchup, onion, dill pickle, dill
pickle juice, horseradish (if using), hot sauce,
Worcestershire sauce, and paprika. Season with
salt and pepper. Use immediately or store in the
refrigerator in an airtight container for up to
1 week.

JOE PEARCE
Slap's BBQ

SPECIALTY: Kansas City–Style Burnt Ends

"Kansas City kind of developed its own style of barbecue," explains Joe Pearce, who runs the popular Slap's BBQ in Kansas City, Kansas. "It all started with a guy named Henry Perry, who was from Texas but spent a lot of time in Memphis before coming to Kansas City, where he refined everything he'd learned from across the southern United States of America."

Thanks to Perry, often called "the father of Kansas City barbecue," Kansas City developed a broadly based barbecue culture. Whereas Texas does brisket, the Carolinas do pork, and Memphis does dry-rubbed ribs, Pearce asserts KC does it all and does it all well.

"Brisket, pork, turkey, sausage, chicken, ribs—all of it," he claims. "But what we're most known for is our burnt ends."

For those who have never experienced the sublime pleasure that comes from eating Kansas City–style burnt ends, which are cut from the fatty point section of beef brisket, Pearce offers this seductive description: "When a brisket cooks low and slow, you get this super-savory, super-tender, caramelized, sweet, salty, beef-flavored piece of meat at the point, because it sits higher in the smoker. Down here, we call burnt ends meat marshmallows."

The crazy thing, adds Pearce, is that back in the early days of Kansas City barbecue, folks didn't know what to do with those dark and forbidding bits of bark-covered beef. In fact, he says, the custom of the day was to trim it off and feed it to the dogs. That's about the time KC's legendary barbecue restaurant Arthur Bryant's, now into its second century, birthed a citywide movement.

"At Arthur Bryant's, there would be these long lines of people waiting for barbecue," he says. "They began handing out the burnt ends as samples, and the next thing you know, they're being sold at every barbecue restaurant across the Kansas City metropolitan area."

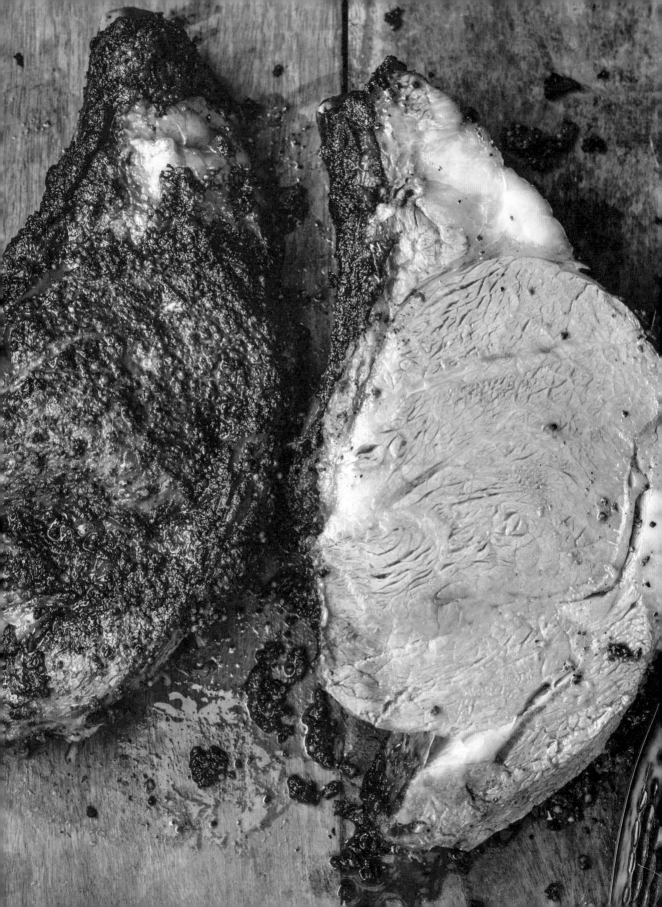

SMOKED PRIME RIB

In my humble opinion, the only thing better than roasted prime rib is smoked prime rib. The seductive flavor of the wood smoke and spice mingles with the flavorful beef to create a dish of epic proportions—trust me. When I'm looking for a real showstopper of a dish to impress guests, this is one of my go-to recipes. This technique calls for a higher smoker temperature and shorter cook time because you don't want to push the meat past medium like you do with regular barbecue, since prime rib is a naturally tender cut.

¼ cup kosher salt

¼ cup freshly ground black pepper

1 tablespoon yellow mustard seeds

1 tablespoon sugar

5 pounds dry-aged bone-in prime rib

3 tablespoons horseradish mustard

1. Prepare and preheat your smoker to 325°F.

2. In a small bowl, mix to combine the salt, pepper, mustard seeds, and sugar. Pat the prime rib dry with paper towels and evenly coat the exterior of the meat with the horseradish mustard. Season on all sides with the spice mixture.

3. When the temperature in the smoker reaches 325°F and the smoke is running clear, add the meat. Cook until the beef reaches an internal temperature of 125°F for rare to 135°F for medium, depending on your desired doneness, about 3½ hours. For the best results, use a probe thermometer to continually monitor the meat's temperature.

4. Transfer the beef to a cutting board and let rest for 20 to 30 minutes. Slice to the desired thickness and serve.

GRILLED SKIRT STEAK TACOS
with Pickled Red Onions

Skirt steak is one of the most flavorful cuts on the entire steer, and when grilled and sliced properly, it's one of the best values at the butcher shop. A hot grill allows you to get a great sear on the meat without pushing it past medium-rare, at which point the meat gets tough. Thinly slice the meat against the grain for the most tender results possible. I like my tacos on the spicy side, so I load them up with plenty of sliced jalapeño and garnish with a squeeze of fresh lime, cilantro, and pickled red onions.

1 tablespoon puréed chipotle in adobo sauce (see Note)

1 tablespoon packed light brown sugar

1 teaspoon ground coriander

1 teaspoon ground cumin

1 tablespoon kosher salt

Juice of 1 lime, plus 2 limes sliced into small wedges

2 pounds skirt steak, trimmed of silver skin

1 package corn tortillas (about 12)

1 bunch cilantro, coarsely chopped

1 jalapeño, thinly sliced into rounds

Pickled Red Onions (recipe follows)

1. In a small bowl, mix to combine the chipotle purée, brown sugar, coriander, cumin, salt, and lime juice. Pat the skirt steak dry with paper towels, place in a zip-top bag, add the chipotle marinade, and toss the meat inside the bag to coat. Marinate in the refrigerator for 1 to 2 hours. Remove the meat from the bag and discard the marinade.

2. Prepare and preheat your lump charcoal grill to high.

3. Place the skirt steak on the grill and cook until medium-rare, about 3 minutes per side.

4. Transfer the steak to a cutting board and let rest for 5 minutes. Thinly slice the meat against the grain and serve with warm or slightly charred corn tortillas, cilantro, jalapeño, pickled onions, and lime wedges.

Note: To make puréed chipotles, blend the entire contents of a 12-ounce can of chipotles in adobo sauce in a blender. What isn't needed can be jarred and refrigerated for up to 3 weeks.

(Recipe continues)

Pickled Red Onions

MAKES 1 QUART

1 pound red onions, halved and thinly sliced

White wine vinegar

Sugar

Kosher salt

2 garlic cloves

1 tablespoon whole black peppercorns

1 tablespoon coriander seeds

½ tablespoon dried red pepper flakes

1 teaspoon yellow mustard seeds

1 fresh bay leaf

Pack the onions into a 1-quart mason jar. Fill the jar with cold water, leaving ½ inch of air space at the top. Pour the water from the jar into a measuring cup (use a spoon to keep the onions in the jar) to calculate its volume. Discard half the water and replace with an equal quantity of vinegar. Add 2 teaspoons sugar and 2 teaspoons salt for every 1 cup liquid.

In a small nonreactive saucepan, combine the vinegar mixture, garlic, peppercorns, coriander seeds, red pepper flakes, mustard seeds, and bay leaf. Bring to a boil over high heat and cook for 2 minutes. Carefully pour the hot liquid over the onions in the jar, seal, and refrigerate for up to 1 month.

As with most things in life, you're only as good as the people around you. That's certainly the case at Mabel's BBQ, where our loyal, hardworking team makes the smoked-meat magic happen every single day.

GRILLED RIB EYE
with Peperonata

When summer is in full swing and I actually have some time to go golfing with my buddies, we almost always end up coming back to my place to eat when we're done. The reason is simple: the guys know I always have some beautiful dry-aged steaks on hand, and that I'm not going to mess them up! Over the years, we've enjoyed a ton of different toppers, like grilled mushrooms and onions or tangy chimichurri. One year my garden overflowed with sweet bell peppers, so it was The Summer of Peperonata! In addition to fruity bell peppers, there's a kick of heat and acid to cut the richness of the steak. The peperonata keeps for a couple of weeks in the fridge, so make a big batch.

2 tablespoons chopped fresh rosemary

2 tablespoons ground fennel seed

2 tablespoons kosher salt

1 tablespoon freshly ground black pepper

4 (1-pound) dry-aged rib eyes

Olive oil

Peperonata (recipe follows)

1. Prepare and preheat your lump charcoal grill to create two heat zones: high and low.

2. In a small bowl, mix to combine the rosemary, fennel, salt, and pepper. Pat the steaks dry with paper towels and season on both sides with the spice mixture. Lightly coat the steaks on all sides with olive oil.

3. Sear the steaks over the hot side of the grill until the exterior forms a nice crust, about 4 minutes per side. Move the meat to the low-heat side of the grill, cover the grill, and cook until the steaks reach an internal temperature of 125°F for rare to 135°F for medium, depending on your desired doneness, about 5 minutes per side.

4. Transfer the steaks to a cutting board and let rest for 10 minutes before serving with peperonata.

(Recipe continues)

Peperonata

MAKES 2 QUARTS

¼ cup olive oil

1 yellow onion, halved and sliced ½-inch thick

1 red bell pepper, sliced ½-inch thick

1 green bell pepper, sliced ½-inch thick

1 yellow bell pepper, sliced ½-inch thick

4 garlic cloves, thinly sliced

1 (15-ounce) can whole peeled tomatoes, crushed by hand

3 sprigs fresh oregano

Pinch of sugar

Kosher salt and freshly ground black pepper

¼ cup jarred Calabrian chiles, drained and sliced

1 tablespoon sherry vinegar

In a large heavy-bottomed skillet, heat the olive oil over medium heat. Add the onion, bell peppers, and garlic and cook, stirring occasionally, until the vegetables are soft and aromatic, about 10 minutes. Add the tomatoes, oregano, and sugar and cook until the peppers are very soft and most of the liquid has evaporated, about 30 minutes. Season with salt and black pepper and stir in the Calabrian chiles and vinegar. Remove and discard the oregano sprigs.

This can be served hot or at room temperature or stored in a jar in the refrigerator for up to 2 weeks.

While you only need to check on smoking meats occasionally, it's vital to monitor and maintain the fire throughout the entire cooking process in order to achieve the ideal levels of heat and smoke.

CHICKEN

FIREPLACE CHICKEN
on a String

If you love tinkering around the house as much as Kyle and I do, this recipe is for you. All you need is a fireplace, two chickens, some butcher's twine, and some courage! We waited until Liz left the house, because she definitely would not have allowed this to go down. This unconventional cooking method creates an incredibly succulent chicken because it is essentially a wood-fired rotisserie bird. To up your game, place a roasting pan of vegetables beneath the birds to roast in all those great drippings. Sure, you could just pop these chickens into a hot oven, but where's the fun and adventure in that?! See opposite for instructions on how to create this setup in your home fireplace.

Butcher's twine

2 (3-pound) whole chickens

2 tablespoons kosher salt

8 sprigs fresh rosemary

10 garlic cloves

1 yellow onion, quartered

2 tablespoons olive oil

1. Soak the butcher's twine in water, making sure to use enough string for the suspension system (see the box, opposite).

2. Pat the chickens dry with paper towels, season inside and out with salt, and refrigerate, uncovered, for at least 1 hour or overnight.

3. Build a nice big fire in your fireplace.

4. Divide the rosemary, garlic, and onion quarters between the chicken cavities. Evenly coat the chickens with the olive oil. Truss the chickens well with the butcher's twine so that the legs and wings are tucked close to the body. Tie lengths of the twine to the legs of the chickens so they will hang neck-side down. Suspend the birds from hooks in the ceiling or mantel (see page 106) so they hang directly in front of the hottest part of the fire. Place a roasting pan beneath the chickens to catch the drippings.

5. Give the birds a gentle twist and they will slowly rotate as they cook. Every 20 minutes or so, moisten the twine with water to prevent it from igniting. If the birds stop turning, give them another gentle twist. Continue feeding the fire to keep it hot.

6. Cook until the chicken reaches an internal temperature of 160°F at the meaty part of the leg, about 90 minutes. Place a platter beneath each bird, cut the twine, loosely tent with aluminum foil, and let them rest for 10 minutes. Carve and serve.

STRING-TURNED ROASTS

This technique for roasting meats like whole chickens, legs of lamb, or boneless pork loins might seem weird—and believe me, Liz certainly thought it was the first time I did it—but it couldn't be more straightforward. You literally just hang a piece of meat on a string in front of the fireplace and watch as it slowly spins and cooks.

That said, there are a few things you need to do to make sure it comes out great.

Before you start cooking, for each roast screw in a sturdy hook on the underside of the mantel, on the face of the mantel, or on the wall or ceiling above the fireplace (every home setup is different) so the piece of meat hanging from it will fall directly in front of the fireplace opening.

It's important to build a nice big fire and let it burn for a while before you start cooking because you want a good base of glowing red embers on the fireplace floor. That's where most of the heat comes from. Keep feeding the fire with new wood throughout the entire cooking process.

Trussing the meat (chicken, leg of lamb, pork loin) with butcher's twine before cooking makes a neat and tidy package that ensures even cooking. It doesn't have to be fancy; just wrap the twine around the meat to secure loose pieces like wings and legs and tie it off (remember that you will be attaching another piece of twine to it, so the trussed meat has to be secure). Your butcher will be happy to truss the meat for you.

Now measure how much additional twine you'll need so the meat will hang from the hook and hover directly in front of the fire. Soak that amount of twine in water for 10 minutes before cooking.

When the fire's good and hot, tie the water-soaked twine to the trussed meat and suspend it from the hook. Place a roasting pan directly beneath the meat to catch those amazing drippings (you can use them to make a gravy, save them to use in place of oil or butter in other recipes, or roast vegetables in them right under the roasting meat). Now give the meat a gentle twist so that it spins lazily in one direction and then the other. When it stops, do it again. Using your fingers, occasionally moisten the twine with water throughout the cooking process so it won't dry, crack, or burn.

Cooking times are approximate because every fire is different. Just check the meat's internal temperature with a thermometer every now and then until it's done. When it is, place a platter directly under the meat, cut the twine, and let the meat rest loosely tented with aluminum foil for about 10 minutes. Slice or carve the meat and serve with those delicious drippings.

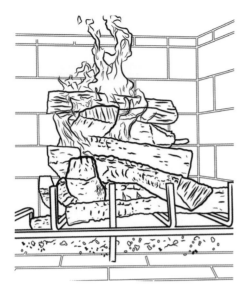

Build a nice big fire and let it burn for a while before you start cooking. You want a good bed of glowing red embers on the fireplace floor.

Attach the trussed chickens to the preinstalled hooks so that the chickens hang directly in front of the fireplace.

Give the chickens a gentle twist so that they spin. Place a roasting pan beneath the chicken to catch the drippings.

Keep feeding the fire, moistening the string, and giving the meat a spin throughout the cooking process.

SPATCHCOCKED BRICK CHICKEN

"Spatchcock" isn't just fun to say—it's an amazing way to cook chicken and turkey because it accomplishes three goals: it speeds up cooking time; results in even cooking, so the breast meat doesn't overcook in the time it takes the dark meat to cook through; and produces perfectly crisp skin. The key to this classic dish from the '80s and '90s is to maintain a steady, moderate heat on the grill so you don't end up with burnt chicken instead of brick chicken! For the juiciest, most flavorful results, season the chicken the night before.

1 (3- to 4-pound) whole chicken

Kosher salt and freshly ground black pepper

Olive oil

1. Place the chicken breast-side down on a cutting board and, using heavy-duty kitchen shears, remove the backbone. Discard the backbone (or save it for stock). Flip the chicken and open it up so it lays flat on the cutting board, skin-side up. Use your palm to press and crack the breastbone so the chicken lies flat. Pat the chicken dry with paper towels, liberally season both sides with salt and pepper, and refrigerate, uncovered, for at least 1 hour but preferably overnight.

2. Prepare and preheat your lump charcoal grill to medium-high. Wrap two bricks in aluminum foil. (In place of bricks you can use heavy cans from the pantry.)

3. Remove the chicken from the refrigerator and allow it to come to room temperature, about 30 minutes. Coat the exterior of the chicken with olive oil. Place the chicken skin-side down on the grill and weigh it down with the two bricks, one over the thighs and the other over the breast. Cook without moving until the skin is nicely charred and crisp, about 10 minutes. Remove the bricks, flip the chicken, return the bricks to the meat, and cover the grill. Cook until the chicken reaches an internal temperature of 160°F at the meaty part of the leg, about 10 minutes.

4. Transfer the chicken to a cutting board and let rest for 10 minutes before quartering and serving.

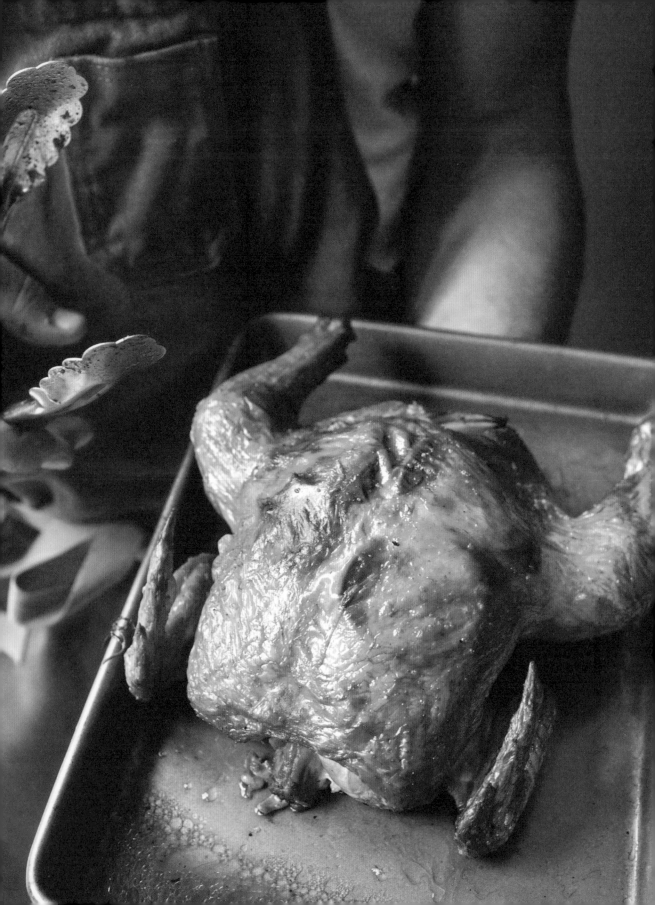

WOOD-ROASTED CHICKEN

One of my all-time favorite dishes is beautifully simple oven-roasted chicken. But something magical happens when you cook whole chickens in a wood-burning oven. If you don't have access to a wood-burning oven, you can do what I do here and use a grill with a cover that is equipped to handle real wood fires. I love this method because the screaming-high but indirect heat cooks the chicken incredibly fast, leaving the meat super juicy and the skin dark, rich, and crispy. For the best results, season the chicken the night before.

1 (3- to 4-pound) whole chicken

1 tablespoon kosher salt

1 lemon, sliced into thin rounds and seeded

2 fresh bay leaves

1 small red onion, quartered

3 garlic cloves

1 small bunch fresh thyme

Olive oil

1. Pat the chicken dry with paper towels, liberally season it inside and out with the salt, and refrigerate, uncovered, for at least 1 hour but preferably overnight.

2. Build a wood fire on one side of the grill.

3. Remove the chicken from the refrigerator and allow it to come to room temperature, about 30 minutes. Lift the skin above each breast and insert 3 lemon slices and 1 bay leaf into the pocket. Put the onion, garlic, thyme, and any remaining lemon slices inside the cavity. Liberally coat the exterior of the chicken with olive oil.

4. When the temperature inside the grill reaches 500°F, lift the cover and place the chicken breast-side up on the side without the fire. Cover and cook until the chicken reaches an internal temperature of 160°F at the meaty part of the leg, about 1 hour.

5. Transfer the chicken to a cutting board and let rest for 10 minutes before carving and serving.

SMOKED WHOLE CHICKEN

I've never been a big fan of brining meat because I find that it alters the texture of the meat—and not in a good way. I was finally convinced to brine whole chickens and turkeys that were headed for the smoker by my good pal Billy Durney from Hometown Bar-B-Que in Red Hook, Brooklyn, who kept telling me to "just brine the damn things!" After countless dry-rub fails, I gave in and learned to love the brine. When it comes to poultry, Billy, you are right. But I'm still not brining anything else!

1 cup pure maple syrup

1 cup kosher salt

3 garlic cloves, smashed

10 sprigs fresh thyme

2 pounds ice (about 6 cups)

1 (3- to 4-pound) whole chicken

3 tablespoons Pork Rub (page 234)

1. In a large stockpot, combine 1 gallon water, the maple syrup, salt, garlic, and thyme. Bring the mixture to a boil over high heat, occasionally stirring to combine the ingredients. Remove the pot from the heat and dump in the ice to quickly cool the contents. Lower the chicken into the brine, keeping it submerged below the surface with a plate weighed down with a heavy can. Refrigerate overnight.

2. Prepare and preheat your smoker to 325°F.

3. Remove the chicken from the brine, pat dry with paper towels, and season inside and out with the pork rub.

4. When the temperature in the smoker reaches 325°F and the smoke is running clear, add the chicken. Cook until the chicken reaches an internal temperature of 160°F at the meaty part of the leg, about 1½ hours. For the best results, use a probe thermometer to continually monitor the meat's temperature.

5. Transfer the chicken to a cutting board, loosely tent it with aluminum foil, and let rest for 10 minutes before carving and serving.

BEER CAN CHICKEN

All hail the king of the backyard grill! I've been making and loving this dish for almost thirty years, ever since I was old enough to drink beer. Back then, of course, we drank cheap beer—and that's still what I recommend using. Sticking a can of fancy craft beer up a chicken seems so wrong. What's great about this recipe is that it requires zero attention while it's cooking, so you and your tailgating buddies can watch the game without interruption and the chicken will still be crisp, juicy, and delicious.

1½ tablespoons garlic salt

1½ tablespoons dried oregano

1 tablespoon ground toasted coriander seeds

1 tablespoon smoked paprika

½ teaspoon kosher salt

1½ teaspoons freshly ground black pepper

1 lemon, halved

1 (3- to 4-pound) whole chicken

1 (12-ounce) can cheap beer

1. In a small bowl, mix to combine the garlic salt, oregano, coriander, paprika, kosher salt, and pepper. Squeeze the lemon halves all over the inside and outside of the chicken. Season the chicken inside and out with the spice mixture and refrigerate, uncovered, for at least 3 hours but preferably overnight.

2. Prepare and preheat your lump charcoal grill to create two heat zones: high and low.

3. Drink one-third of the beer. Place the chicken on top of the beer can, sliding the can up and into the cavity of the bird. Set the bird upright and coat the chicken in olive oil. Position the chicken on the low-heat side of the grill, using the beer can and legs to stabilize it. Cover and cook until the chicken reaches an internal temperature of 160°F at the meaty part of the leg, about 45 minutes.

4. Remove the chicken from the grill, loosely tent with aluminum foil, and let rest for 10 minutes. Carefully remove the beer can (discard the warm beer), carve, and serve.

Drink or pour off one-third of a can of beer and then slide the can up and into the cavity of the bird.

Position the chicken on the low-heat side of the grill, using the beer can and chicken legs to stabilize it. Cover the grill.

Occasionally check the meat's temperature with a thermometer.

When the chicken is done, remove it from the grill, loosely tent with aluminum foil, and let rest for 10 minutes.

FIRE-BRAISED CHICKEN
Barbacoa

One of my favorite pieces of cooking equipment is a sturdy cast-iron pot. Not only are they rock-solid enough to go straight into a hot fire, they are affordable and will last for generations. This recipe can be made indoors in a fireplace, outdoors in a fire pit, or in a grill equipped to handle real wood fires. Build a nice big fire and wait until it burns down to a thick bed of glowing embers before you start.

1 (3-pound) chicken, cut into 8 pieces

1 tablespoon kosher salt

1 tablespoon freshly ground black pepper

2 tablespoons chicken schmaltz or olive oil

4 garlic cloves, smashed

1 yellow onion, quartered

1 tablespoon cumin seeds

2 (12-ounce) beers, preferably IPA style

3 tablespoons puréed chipotles in adobo sauce (see Note, page 92)

1 teaspoon fresh oregano leaves

Corn tortillas or steamed rice, for serving

Lime wedges, for serving

Fresh cilantro leaves, for serving

1. Build a nice big wood fire in a fireplace, fire pit, or grill.

2. Pat the chicken pieces dry with paper towels and season with the salt and pepper.

3. When the wood has burned down to a hot bed of glowing embers, place a large cast-iron pot directly onto the coals. When the pot is hot, about 5 minutes, add the schmaltz or olive oil and brown the chicken on all sides, about 2 minutes per side. Add the garlic and onion and cook until softened, about 2 minutes. Stir in the cumin and cook for 1 minute. Add the beer, chipotle purée, and oregano. Let the chicken simmer in the sauce until it reaches an internal temperature of 160°F at the meaty part of the leg, about 45 minutes.

4. Carefully remove the pot from the fire. Remove the chicken pieces from the pot and set them on a cutting board. Once they are cool enough to handle, pull all the meat off the bones and lightly shred the meat. Discard the skin and bones, return the shredded chicken to the pot, and stir to combine.

5. Serve with charred corn tortillas (or steamed rice), lime wedges, and cilantro.

GRILLED CHICKEN THIGHS
with Blackberry BBQ Sauce

I'm not gonna lie: when it comes to chicken, I'm definitely a thigh guy! To me, skin-on, bone-in chicken thighs have more flavor than any other part of the bird. If you moderate the grill temperature to cook them evenly, they are impossible to beat, making chicken thighs my favorite part of the bird. I love pairing grilled chicken with a fruit-based barbecue sauce. This one has fresh blackberries that add a subtle sweetness to the sauce, balance out the heat of the chiles, and soften the acidity of the vinegars.

1 tablespoon ground coriander

1 tablespoon smoked paprika

1 tablespoon kosher salt

8 skin-on, bone-in chicken thighs

Olive oil

½ recipe Blackberry BBQ Sauce
(recipe follows)

1. In a small bowl, mix to combine the coriander, paprika, and salt. Pat the chicken thighs dry with paper towels, season on both sides with the spice mixture, and place in a gallon-size zip-top bag. Refrigerate for several hours but preferably overnight.

2. Prepare and preheat your lump charcoal grill to create two heat zones: high and low.

3. Brush the chicken thighs with olive oil and place them skin-side down on the hot side of the grill. Cover and cook for 2 minutes. Remove the cover and move the chicken to the low-heat side of the grill, skin-side up. Cover and cook until the thighs reach an internal temperature of 160°F, about 15 minutes. Pour half the sauce into a medium bowl and use it to baste the chicken occasionally during the final 10 minutes of cooking.

4. Remove the chicken from the grill and serve with the remaining sauce on the side.

(Recipe continues)

Blackberry BBQ Sauce

MAKES 2 QUARTS

3 pints fresh blackberries

1 (12-ounce) dark beer

1 cup balsamic vinegar

1 cup red wine vinegar

½ cup packed light brown sugar

1 onion, sliced

1 garlic clove, minced

1 habanero pepper, slit

1 tablespoon ground chipotle chile powder

1 tablespoon finely ground coffee

1 tablespoon ground coriander

1 tablespoon ground cumin

In a large saucepan, combine the blackberries, beer, balsamic vinegar, red wine vinegar, sugar, onion, garlic, habanero pepper, chipotle, coffee, coriander, and cumin and cook over medium-low heat, stirring occasionally, for 2 hours. Remove the pan from the heat and carefully blend or purée the sauce in a blender or food processor until smooth. Strain the sauce and set aside until needed.

Use immediately or store in the refrigerator for up to 2 weeks.

My preference is to always use skin-on, bone-in proteins, and chicken thighs
are no exception. Don't be afraid to use seasonal fruit in sauces and glazes,
but make sure you wait until the end of the cooking process to apply them so
you don't end up with a charred mess!

CAMPFIRE MOLE CHICKEN

I absolutely love the flavor and aroma of real Mexican mole. It has an exotic quality to it from the nuts, chiles, spices, and bitter Mexican chocolate. The result is a deeply complex sauce that is rich, multidimensional, and unforgettable. I know the ingredient list looks long and intimidating, but I think you'll agree that the results are worth the effort. Save this recipe for a special dinner with family or friends. I like to serve this dish over steamed rice with plenty of fresh cilantro and Spicy Marinated Onions (page 126).

3 (6-inch) corn tortillas

4 dried pasilla chiles, stemmed and seeded

3 dried ancho chilies, stemmed and seeded

½ cup dark raisins

3 cups boiling water

1 (3- to 4-pound) chicken, cut into 8 pieces

1 tablespoon kosher salt, plus more as needed

Freshly ground black pepper

Olive oil

2 small red onions, diced

4 garlic cloves, coarsely chopped

¼ cup sliced almonds

¼ cup hulled pumpkin seeds

¼ cup white sesame seeds

2 teaspoons coriander seeds

2 teaspoons dried oregano

1 teaspoon cumin seeds

2½ cups chicken stock

1 large tomato, cored and coarsely chopped

1 cup fresh orange juice

2 strips orange zest, peeled with a vegetable peeler

1 cinnamon stick

2 discs (one 2.7-ounce package) Mexican chocolate

Juice of 1 lime

Steamed rice, for serving

Chopped fresh cilantro, for serving

Spicy Marinated Onions (recipe follows)

(Recipe continues)

1. Build a nice big wood fire in a fireplace, fire pit, or grill.

2. Char the tortillas on both sides over the flames, about 2 minutes per side. When cool enough to handle, shred the tortillas into medium pieces. In a medium bowl, combine the tortillas, chiles, raisins, and boiling water. Cover with plastic wrap and set aside for 5 minutes for the chiles to soften. Strain and reserve the liquid. In a blender, combine the chile mixture and ¾ cup of the reserved chile soaking liquid (discard the rest). Purée until smooth and set aside.

3. Pat the chicken pieces dry with paper towels and season liberally with the salt and black pepper.

4. When the wood has burned down to a nice hot bed of glowing embers, place a large cast-iron pot directly onto the coals. When the pot is hot, about 5 minutes, add enough olive oil to coat the bottom of the pot and brown the chicken on all sides, about 2 minutes per side. Transfer the chicken to a platter and set aside.

5. To the same pan, add the onions, garlic, and a pinch of salt and cook for 1 minute. Add the almonds, pumpkin seeds, sesame seeds, coriander, oregano, and cumin and cook for 1 minute. Add the stock, tomato, orange juice, and chile purée and bring to a simmer.

6. Carefully pour the contents of the pan into a blender, purée until smooth, and return it to the pan. Add the orange zest, cinnamon stick, and chicken and cook, uncovered, until the chicken reaches an internal temperature of 160°F at the meaty part of the leg, about 45 minutes. Remove the chicken from the pan and set aside.

7. Remove the pan from the heat, discard the orange zest and cinnamon stick, and stir in the chocolate and lime juice. Carefully pull and shred the chicken meat (discarding the skin and bones), return it to the pot, and stir to combine.

8. Serve over steamed rice with cilantro and spicy marinated onions.

Spicy Marinated Onions

¾ cup fresh orange juice

½ cup fresh lime juice

1 large red onion, thinly sliced

2 jalapeños, thinly sliced into rings

Kosher salt

In a small bowl, whisk together the orange juice and lime juice. Add the onion and jalapeños and stir to combine. Season with salt, cover with plastic wrap, and allow the onion to soften and marinate until needed. Use immediately or store in the refrigerator in an airtight container for up to 2 weeks.

CHICKEN IN HAY

While this technique might sound odd, the use of hay (dried grass) imparts a sweet and subtle smokiness to food that isn't as overpowering as many traditional smoked meats. This recipe also is perfect on those frigid winter nights when you don't feel like going outside to fire up the smoker, because it works great indoors in a hot oven. Feel free to experiment with different meats, because they all take on interesting flavors from the hay. I get hay at the local farmers' market, but you can also order it online.

1 (3- to 4-pound) chicken

1 tablespoon kosher salt

2 cups cider vinegar

2 tablespoons unsalted butter

12 by 12-inch piece of cheesecloth

6 fresh bay leaves

12 garlic cloves, unpeeled

Large bunch of clean hay

1. Prepare and preheat your lump charcoal grill for indirect cooking, with one hot side and one hold (unheated) side.

2. Set the chicken on a cutting board and pat dry with paper towels. Liberally season inside and out with the salt.

3. In a medium saucepan, combine the vinegar and butter over medium heat. Once the butter melts, remove the pan from the heat and stir to combine. Dunk the cheesecloth in the saucepan to absorb the liquid.

4. Arrange 4 bay leaves and 6 garlic cloves on top of the chicken and insert the remaining bay leaves and garlic into the cavity of the bird. Wrap the chicken with the butter-soaked cheesecloth and set it aside.

5. Line a large roasting pan with the hay, place the chicken on the hay, and cover the bird with more hay. Put the chicken on the hold side of the grill, cover, and cook until the chicken reaches an internal temperature of 160°F at the meaty part of the leg, about 90 minutes. For the best results, use a probe thermometer to continually monitor the meat's temperature.

6. Remove the chicken from the grill and let rest for 10 minutes.

7. Remove the chicken from the hay and cheesecloth, carve, and serve.

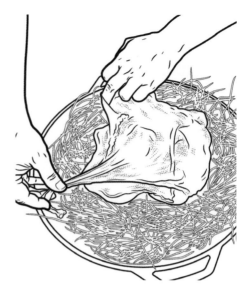

Line a large roasting pan with the hay, place the chicken with the butter-soaked cheesecloth on the hay and set the chicken on top. Arrange 4 bay leaves and 6 garlic cloves on top of the chicken.

Insert the remaining bay leaves and garlic into the cavity of the bird and then wrap the cheesecloth over the chicken to completely enclose it.

Cover the bird with more hay, put the chicken on the unheated side of the grill, and cover the grill.

When the chicken is done, remove it from the grill, and let it rest for 10 minutes before removing the hay and cheesecloth.

SEAFOOD

SPICY GRILLED SHRIMP TOAST
with Avocado

When summer rolls around, Liz and I like to spend as much time as possible outside, and that includes when entertaining friends. We're always looking for foods that we can cook on the grill (or in the smoker) so we don't miss out on any of the fun. This dish is one of the biggest hits because it's savory, crunchy, and creamy. And best of all, you can eat the shrimp with one hand, leaving the other free for a glass of chilled white wine. Use good-quality peasant bread and feel free to add any fresh herbs from the garden into the avocado mixture. If using wooden skewers to grill the shrimp, soak them in water for at least 30 minutes to prevent flames.

¼ cup olive oil, plus extra for grilling the bread

½ teaspoon ground coriander

½ teaspoon crushed red pepper flakes

Zest and juice of 1 lime

1 pound medium shrimp, peeled and deveined

2 avocados, halved, pitted, and peeled

1 garlic clove, minced

1 large tomato, diced

2 tablespoons finely chopped fresh cilantro leaves

1 jalapeño, minced

Kosher salt

1 loaf peasant bread, cut into ½-inch-thick slices

1. Prepare and preheat your lump charcoal grill to high.

2. In a medium bowl, whisk to combine the olive oil, coriander, red pepper flakes, and lime zest. Add the shrimp and toss to coat. Cover and refrigerate until needed (but no longer than 8 hours).

3. In a large bowl, smash the avocado flesh with a fork or potato masher. Add the lime juice, garlic, tomato, cilantro, and jalapeño and stir to combine. Season with salt.

4. Brush both sides of the bread with olive oil and grill until nicely toasted and grill-marked, about 30 seconds per side.

5. Season the shrimp on both sides with salt, thread onto skewers, and grill until just cooked through, about 2 minutes per side. Remove the shrimp from the grill, pull off the skewers, and chop into bite-size pieces.

6. To assemble the toasts, spread a heaping tablespoon of the avocado mixture onto the bread and top with a few spoonfuls of the shrimp.

GRILLED WALLEYE
Wrapped in Corn Husks

When most people think of cooking with corn husks, they naturally think of steamed tamales. I love using them for all kinds of things, but especially grilling delicate lake fish like walleye or perch, which are freshwater fish common to the Great Lakes region. They help keep the fish from drying out, but also hold in sauces like this zippy lime and cilantro butter, which bastes the fish as it cooks. Since the Midwest happens to have plenty of lake fish and plenty of corn, this recipe makes perfect sense. I buy my husks from the Mexican market, but many groceries now stock them in the ethnic foods aisle.

8 dried corn husks

1½ cups (3 sticks) unsalted butter, softened

1 poblano pepper, seeded and minced

1 small shallot, minced

Zest and juice of 1 lime

2 tablespoons finely chopped fresh cilantro leaves

1 teaspoon kosher salt

3 pounds boneless, skinless walleye fillets

1. Soak the corn husks in water overnight, keeping them submerged below the surface with a plate weighed down with a heavy can.

2. Prepare and preheat your lump charcoal grill for indirect cooking, with one hot side and one hold (unheated) side.

3. In a medium bowl, mix to combine the butter, poblano, shallot, lime zest, lime juice, cilantro, and salt.

4. Drain the water from the corn husks and arrange them flat on a work surface. Divide the fish into 8 equal portions and place them on the husks. Top each fish with an equal portion of the butter mixture. Fold the sides of the husks over the fish to form a cylinder and then fold up or tie the ends to form a small bundle (like a tamale).

5. Put the husk packages on the hold side of the grill, cover, and cook until the fish reaches an internal temperature of 140°F, about 12 minutes. Remove from the grill, open the packets (careful—the steam will be hot), and serve.

GRILLED SWORDFISH
Agrodolce

When I started in the restaurant business as a teenage cook at Sammy's in Cleveland, we couldn't stock enough swordfish to keep up with demand. We obviously were not alone, as the demand for swordfish soon outpaced supply. But after many years, when responsible chefs would not sell swordfish because of overfishing, things improved dramatically for the fish. That's great news, because it's one of my favorites. During a trip to Sicily, we literally watched a fisherman walk a fresh-caught swordfish from his boat to the market. When we got the fish back to the house, this is the dish that Bobby Flay made us. It was the most delicious piece of fish I have ever eaten, and the plum agrodolce sauce served with it was the perfect match.

1 cup honey

4 cups red wine vinegar

3 cups halved, pitted, and sliced black plums

Kosher salt and freshly ground black pepper

1 tablespoon brined capers, drained and rinsed

2 tablespoons cold unsalted butter, cut into small pieces

2 tablespoons finely chopped fresh mint leaves, plus whole leaves for garnish

4 (1-inch-thick) swordfish steaks

1 tablespoon olive oil

1. Prepare and preheat your lump charcoal grill to create two heat zones: high and low.

2. Place a medium nonreactive saucepan on the low side of the grill. Combine the honey, vinegar, and 2 cups of the plums and cook, stirring occasionally, until the liquid has reduced by half to a thick-sauce consistency, about 10 minutes. Season with salt and pepper. Strain through a fine-mesh sieve into a bowl (discarding solids), add the capers, butter, and mint, and stir to combine.

3. Meanwhile, pat the swordfish steaks dry with paper towels, season both sides with salt and pepper, and lightly coat with the olive oil. Sear the swordfish over the hot side of the grill until the exterior forms a nice crust and the fish reaches an internal temperature of 130°F, about 3 minutes per side.

4. When the swordfish is done, transfer it to a platter, spoon over the plum sauce, and garnish with the remaining plum slices and mint. Serve with extra sauce on the side.

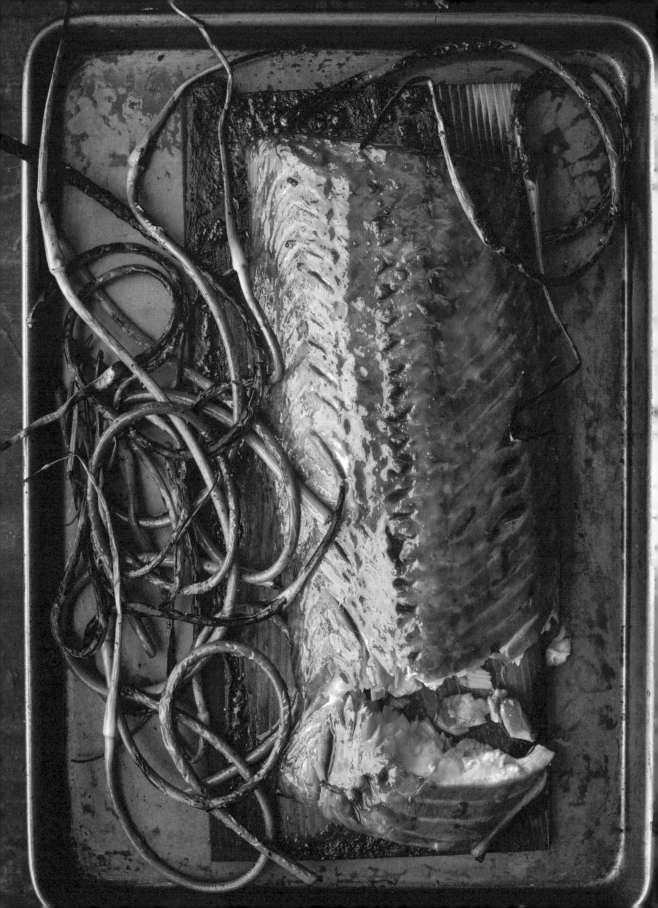

CEDAR-PLANKED SALMON

This a great method not only to cook the salmon but to serve it as well, because there's something pretty cool about presenting a large, beautiful piece of fish on a fragrant cedar plank. As the wood absorbs heat from the grill, it transfers a pleasant woodsy aroma to the fish. This technique also eliminates the need to flip the fish, which is always a little bit tricky on the grill. I like to use a straightforward sweet mustard glaze to highlight the natural salmon and wood flavors. For a great brunch dish, serve with a nice seasonal salad.

1 large cedar plank

1 cup soy sauce

2 tablespoons honey

1 tablespoon Dijon mustard

1 tablespoon olive oil

1 bunch scallions or garlic scapes, ends trimmed

Kosher salt and freshly ground black pepper

1 (3- to 5-pound) skin-on side of salmon

1. Soak the cedar plank in water for at least 2 hours.

2. Prepare and preheat your lump charcoal grill to create two heat zones: high and low.

3. In a small saucepan, combine the soy sauce and honey and cook over medium-high heat, stirring occasionally, until reduced by half, about 3 minutes. Remove from the heat and stir in the mustard.

4. Drizzle the olive oil on the scallions, season with salt and pepper, and put on the hot side of the grill. Cook until the scallions are bright green and lightly charred, about 2 minutes per side. Remove from the grill and set aside until needed.

5. Brush the soy glaze on both sides of the salmon. Put the salmon skin-side down on the cedar plank, place it on the low-heat side of the grill, cover the grill, and cook until the fish reaches an internal temperature of 130°F, about 25 minutes.

6. Serve the salmon on the cedar plank with the scapes or scallions on the side.

WHOLE GRILLED STRIPED BASS

I love to toss the whole fish—skin, head, and tail—right on the grill. The skin helps to keep the fish from drying out, the bones add a ton of flavor, and the presentation is stunning and impressive. Sure, some people are bound to be a little freaked out by the eyeballs, but I say, go for it! If you can't look your food straight in the eye, maybe it's time to make the switch to vegetarianism!

2 (3-pound) whole striped bass, gutted and scaled

Kosher salt and freshly ground black pepper

4 lemons, sliced

2 bundles fresh dill

Olive oil

1. Prepare and preheat your lump charcoal grill to medium-high.

2. Pat the fish dry with paper towels and season inside and out with salt and pepper. With a sharp knife, make three or four shallow diagonal slits (about 3 inches long and ¼ inch deep) into the flesh of the fish on each side. Insert the lemon and dill into the cavity of each fish and coat the exterior with olive oil.

3. Scrub and oil the grill grates, put the fish on the grill, and cook until the fish reaches an internal temperature of 140°F, about 10 minutes per side, depending on thickness. Transfer the fish to a platter and serve.

SMOKED WHITEFISH PÂTÉ

Whenever I'm lucky enough to sneak away from work and visit chef Mario Batali up in northern Michigan, where he often vacations with his family, we always go to Carlson's Fishery in Leland, an active fishing village. Carlson's, a hundred-year-old family business, operates smokehouses that turn out the most amazing fish jerky, whitefish sausage, and smoked whitefish. My favorite is their smoked fish pâté, which is delicious as a dip or a schmear on a warm bagel or slice of toasted pumpernickel garnished with caper berries and celery leaves.

1 cup packed light brown sugar

1½ cups kosher salt

1 (3-pound) boneless, skin-on whitefish fillet

½ cup mayonnaise

½ cup plain Greek yogurt

2 scallions, thinly sliced

1 tablespoon Dijon mustard

1 tablespoon sweet paprika

½ teaspoon celery seeds

4 to 8 slices pumpernickel bread, for serving

1 lemon, cut into wedges, for serving

Caper berries, for serving

Whole celery leaves, for serving

1. In a large container, mix to fully combine 3 gallons ice-cold water, the brown sugar, and the salt. Refrigerate until cool. Add the fish to the brine and refrigerate for 4 hours.

2. Prepare and preheat your smoker to 250°F. When the temperature reaches 250°F and the smoke is running clear, remove the fish from the brine (discard the brine), rinse the fish off with cold water, pat it dry with paper towels, and put it in the smoker. Cook until the fish reaches an internal temperature of 140°F, about 3 hours. For the best results, use a probe thermometer to continually monitor the fish's temperature.

3. In a large bowl, mix to combine the mayonnaise, yogurt, scallions, mustard, paprika, and celery seeds. Remove and discard the skin from the smoked fish. Using a pair of forks, shred the fish into large flakes and add them to the bowl. Gently fold the fish into the mayonnaise mixture to combine. Use immediately or store in the refrigerator in an airtight container for up to 1 week. Serve with the pumpernickel bread, lemon, caper berries, and celery leaves.

SMOKED STURGEON

There was a time when the Great Lakes were teeming with giant sturgeons. Can you imagine if Cleveland became the caviar capital of the world? These days, most of the sturgeon we eat is fished along the Atlantic Coast, but that doesn't change the fact that these prehistoric-looking creatures—they grow up to eight feet long and have armor!—are one of the best types of fish for the smoker. Just like wild salmon, these fish are rich, firm, and fatty, making them ideal for this preparation. If you have spring onions—or even a quartered onion—grill to serve alongside the sturgeon.

½ cup bourbon

1 cup kosher salt

½ cup packed light brown sugar

1 teaspoon ground mustard

¼ teaspoon ground mace

1 (3-pound) boneless, skinless sturgeon fillet (swordfish or mahi-mahi also work)

Olive oil

Capers, for serving

1 lemon, cut into wedges, for serving

1. In a small bowl, mix to combine the bourbon, salt, sugar, ground mustard, and mace. Pat the sturgeon dry with paper towels and season on all sides with the spice mixture. Wrap the fish in plastic wrap and refrigerate overnight.

2. Prepare and preheat your smoker to 180°F. When the temperature reaches 180°F and the smoke is running clear, rinse the fish off with cold water, pat it dry with paper towels, and put it in the smoker.

3. Cook until the fish reaches an internal temperature of 140°F, about 4 hours. For the best results, use a probe thermometer to continually monitor the fish's temperature.

4. Slice or flake the fish with a fork, drizzle with olive oil, and serve warm or cold with the capers and lemon.

FIREPLACE CLAMS
with Sauerkraut and Bacon

I know that we usually enjoy clams steamed, fried, with pasta, or in a chowder. But this recipe will forever change your mind on when and how to prepare them. I make this dish in the winter months, when I have a nice fire going and I don't feel like turning on the stove. Listening to the bacon sizzle and watching those clams pop open in my fireplace from the comfort of my couch brings me so much joy, you can't even believe it. The addition of sauerkraut and hard cider rounds out the dish and really puts it over the top.

½ pound bacon, diced

1 teaspoon cumin seeds

1 jalapeño, thinly sliced into rounds

1 small yellow onion, sliced

1 teaspoon kosher salt

2 dozen littleneck clams, cleaned

1 cup sauerkraut, homemade (page 206) or store-bought

1 cup hard cider (or Champagne, if you're feeling fancy)

Crusty bread, for serving

1. Build a nice big wood fire in a fireplace, fire pit, or grill.

2. When the wood has burned down to a hot bed of glowing embers, place a large cast-iron pot directly onto the coals. Immediately add the bacon and cook, stirring occasionally, for 2 minutes. Add the cumin seeds and cook for 1 minute. Add the jalapeño, onion, and salt and cook until the onion is tender, about 2 minutes. Add the clams and cook for 2 minutes. Add the sauerkraut and cider and cook until the clams open, about 8 minutes. Discard any clams that do not open.

3. Serve with plenty of crusty bread.

LAMB

GRILLED LAMB CHOPS
with Lavender Salt

Lamb and lavender is a magical combination that is tough to beat. But there doesn't seem to be any food that lavender salt doesn't make better, which is why I make double and triple batches of the stuff. The salt keeps for months in an airtight container and goes great with grilled lamb, chicken, and even fish. Also, feel free to experiment by substituting the lavender with various dried herbs like rosemary, thyme, and mint.

2 tablespoons dried lavender

½ cup flaky sea salt, like Maldon

24 (4-ounce) domestic lamb chops, frenched (have your butcher do this)

Olive oil

A handful of blackberries, for serving

1. Rub the lavender between your fingers to release the natural oils. In a small bowl, mix to combine the lavender and salt.

2. Prepare and preheat your lump charcoal grill to medium-high.

3. Allow the lamb chops to come to room temperature, about 30 minutes. Pat the chops dry with paper towels and thoroughly coat the exterior with olive oil. Put on the grill and cook until the exterior forms a nice crust and the lamb reaches an internal temperature of 135°F, about 3 minutes per side. Remove the chops from the grill, drizzle with olive oil, season on both sides with the lavender salt, garnish with fresh blackberries, and serve immediately.

GRILLED LAMB SOUVLAKI

Souvlaki is the Greek name for all sorts of grilled-meat kebabs, and they're the perfect foods for backyard barbecues. The great thing about souvlaki is that you can make them with any kind of meat, or even with fish and vegetables. You don't have to use expensive cuts of meat; in fact, I prefer the wallet-friendly shoulder of lamb and pork, and chicken and turkey thighs. The marinade I pair with lamb shoulder here helps tenderize the meat while adding tons of flavor. Try not to cook these too hot and too fast, as they come out much better over moderate, steady heat.

6 tablespoons olive oil

6 tablespoons red wine vinegar

3 tablespoons finely chopped fresh oregano leaves, plus more for garnish

2 garlic cloves, minced

Zest and juice of 2 lemons, plus lemon wedges for serving

1 (3-pound) lamb shoulder, trimmed of excess fat and cut into 1-inch cubes

1 tablespoon kosher salt

1. In a medium bowl, whisk to combine the olive oil, vinegar, oregano, garlic, lemon zest, and lemon juice. Place the lamb in a gallon-size zip-top bag, add the marinade, and toss the meat inside the bag to coat. Refrigerate for several hours or up to overnight.

2. If using wooden skewers, soak them in water for at least 30 minutes to prevent flames.

3. Prepare and preheat your lump charcoal grill to create two heat zones: high and low.

4. Remove the lamb from the bag and discard the marinade. Thread the lamb pieces evenly on the skewers and season with the salt. Sear the lamb over the hot side of the grill until the exterior forms a nice crust, about 8 minutes per side. Move the lamb to the low-heat side of the grill, cover the grill, and cook until the meat reaches an internal temperature of 160°F, about 10 minutes longer. Transfer to a large platter and serve with lemon wedges.

BILLY DURNEY
Hometown Bar-B-Que

SPECIALTY: New York–Style Lamb Belly Banh Mi

Hometown Bar-B-Que is considered to be one of the best barbecue restaurants in the world. That's quite a distinction, considering that the restaurant is based in Brooklyn and was founded by a career-changing owner with no previous professional culinary experience. Since opening his shop in 2013, Billy Durney has been wowing fans with his barbecue, which some are referring to as New York or Brooklyn style.

"I definitely pay tribute to Texas-style barbecue, but the most important thing when talking about this new, New York–style barbecue is the fact that we have no rules," Durney explains. "As long as you're cooking with real wood from start to finish, you get to manipulate the flavors to whatever you want them to be."

While a guy like West Tennessee–based Patrick Martin would "get strung up by his feet" for veering even minimally from whole-hog barbecue, Durney says that his location gives him license to create lust-worthy but unorthodox dishes like smoked lamb belly banh mi sandwiches and Korean-style sticky ribs.

"A lot of these dishes are based on my memories of growing up with the most ethnically diverse multicultural cuisine in the world," he says. "Those Korean-style sticky ribs are an homage to the Chinese place I was hitting after hours as an eighteen-year-old kid. I'm putting my soul on the plate and taking people on a journey of where I've been and what those taste memories mean to me."

To make those banh mi sandwiches, Durney rubs bone-in lamb breasts with salt, pepper, and turbinado sugar and allows them to cure overnight. He smokes them for about 10 hours at a very low 210°F, until you can "pull the bones out like a loose tooth." The wood he uses is mainly white oak, but he finishes the meat with cherry wood. "You don't want it to be overbearing, just the fourth or fifth ingredient," he explains. The succulent meat is chopped, placed on a buttered and grilled baguette, and topped with a pickled daikon and carrot slaw, cilantro, and Vietnamese hot sauce.

Those sandwiches, along with Hometown's exceptional beef brisket, beef ribs, and pork spareribs, attract long lines and a broad clientele, which confirms that he's on the right path.

"What I'm most proud of is when the best chefs in New York started eating at Hometown, because they don't eat at places for hipness, they are always seeking out the best in its class," he says.

GRILLED LAMB SHOULDER
Avgolemono

I know that lamb chops get all the love, but lamb shoulder is a fantastic and inexpensive cut of meat that deserves some attention. When cooked and sliced properly, the meat is tender, juicy, and deeply flavorful. When cooked and sliced improperly, the meat can be tough, dry, and chewy. After a good, hot sear to develop a crust, you want to cook the shoulder low and slow over indirect heat. After it's done cooking, allow the meat to rest before slicing it against the grain. The Greek-style egg and lemon sauce adds a nice lift to the meat. I like to serve this with roasted potatoes.

½ cup olive oil

2 tablespoons red wine vinegar

3 garlic cloves, minced

2 tablespoons plus ½ teaspoon kosher salt

2 tablespoons freshly ground black pepper

2 tablespoons ground fennel seed

1 tablespoon crushed red pepper flakes

1 (5- to 6-pound) whole boneless lamb shoulder

1 cup chicken stock

2 large egg yolks

Juice of 2 lemons

¼ cup finely chopped fresh dill

1 teaspoon cornstarch

1. Prepare and preheat your lump charcoal grill for indirect cooking, with one hot side and one hold (unheated) side.

2. In a medium bowl, whisk to combine the olive oil, vinegar, two-thirds of the garlic, 2 tablespoons of the salt, the black pepper, fennel seed, and red pepper flakes. Pat the lamb dry with paper towels and coat on all sides with half of this mixture, reserving the other half for basting.

3. Sear the lamb over the hot side of the grill until the exterior forms a nice crust, about 8 minutes per side. Move the lamb to the hold side of the grill, cover, and cook until the meat reaches an internal temperature of 180°F, about 2 hours, basting it with the reserved marinade every 15 minutes.

4. Meanwhile, in a medium saucepan, bring the chicken stock to a simmer over medium-high heat. In a separate bowl, whisk to combine the egg yolks, lemon juice, dill, remaining garlic, cornstarch, and remaining ½ teaspoon salt. When the chicken stock reaches a simmer, slowly add it to the egg mixture, whisking the entire time. When fully combined, return the sauce to the saucepan over low heat to keep warm.

5. Remove the lamb from the grill and let rest for about 25 minutes. Slice the meat against the grain, drizzle with the warm sauce, and serve.

SMOKED LAMB RIBS
with Lemon and Honey

This is a dish my family has been making and loving for ages—long before Mabel's BBQ was even a vision in my mind. We used to prepare the ribs in a classic Greek style on the grill, but when we began planning Mabel's, I knew I wanted to serve a true smoked lamb rib. The first time we tested them out was at the Music City Food + Wine Festival in Nashville. Venues like that are awesome places to try out new dishes because you get immediate feedback from literally thousands of diners in a very short time. Our line soon grew to several hundred people long, which let me know that it was probably a good idea to go ahead and put them on the menu.

6 (1- to 2-pound) racks lamb spareribs

1 cup Lamb Rub (page 234)

¼ cup fresh lemon juice

¼ cup honey

2 tablespoons fresh oregano leaves

1. Prepare and preheat your smoker to 300°F.

2. Pat the lamb ribs dry with paper towels and season on both sides with the lamb rub. When the temperature in the smoker reaches 300°F and the smoke is running clear, add the ribs meaty-side up. After 1 hour, test the ribs for doneness by flipping a rack and pressing the meat between the bones. If the meat pulls away from the bones, it's done. If not, continue smoking until it does, about 15 minutes more.

3. Meanwhile, in a small bowl, whisk to combine the lemon juice, honey, and oregano. When the ribs are done, remove them from the smoker and gently brush them with this mixture, being careful not to remove the beautiful bark that forms on the exterior. Cut between the bones and serve with Cucumber Salad (page 202).

PAT BOSLEY

Moonlite Bar-B-Q

SPECIALTY: Western Kentucky Barbecue Mutton

As a food product, mutton has long been regarded as being inferior to lamb and, well, pretty much every other type of meat that's commonly consumed in the United States. That is, unless you happen to live in Owensboro, Kentucky, where the uncommon meat forms the backbone of that region's proud, long-standing barbecue tradition. In Western Kentucky, "barbecue" means slow-cooked mutton.

"The Welsh Catholics who settled Daviess County brought the mutton tradition with them," explains Pat Bosley, third-generation pitmaster at Moonlite Bar-B-Q. "At small family farms, the female ewe that wasn't lambing anymore would be slaughtered, barbecued, and served at a big church or family get-together. The tradition mainly stayed alive thanks to church picnics."

It wasn't just the decline of the rural lifestyle that all but killed off the taste for mutton. Bosley says that the meat earned its less-than-favorable reputation around the time of World War II, when GIs overseas were fed a steady diet of boiled canned mutton. When they returned home, the meat was forbidden food at most households.

"Boiled mutton smelled and tasted awful," he explains. "That's the worst way to cook it and that turned a lot of people off of mutton."

Things are very different at Moonlite, where the popular restaurant flies through about six thousand pounds of mutton per week, which is actually down from a peak of about fifteen thousand pounds. Given that the Moonlite has been skillfully preparing mutton since 1963, when Pat's grandparents, Catherine and Hugh "Pappy" Bosley Sr., opened up shop, it's no surprise that the mouth-watering barbecue attracts fans from miles away.

Technically, Bosley explains, mutton comes from sheep that are one to five years old (any younger, and it's considered lamb), but they are very particular when it comes to sourcing what gets served at the restaurant.

"We use two-year-old female sheep because it tends to be more tender, less gamey, and has a nice fat cap to protect it during the long cooking," he says.

After trimming off the necks and shanks, which go into another regional specialty, burgoo stew, the hundred-pound carcasses are cut into quarters, seasoned with salt and pepper, and slowly cooked over hickory wood for 12 to 15 hours. The large pieces of meat are rotated front to back and top to bottom to achieve even cooking, and they are continually basted with sauce.

"It's a thin Worcestershire and vinegar sauce, which we call dip, and it's another thing that sets Western Kentucky apart," Bosley notes.

At the Moonlite, mutton is served as four main cuts. The most popular is the shoulder, which gets chopped with a cleaver and mixed with dip. The leaner mutton hams and loins are cut on a band saw into slices. And mutton ribs, a rich, fatty delicacy adored by old-timers, are sold by the pound.

Thanks to mutton, Moonlite Bar-B-Q has mushroomed over the years from 20 seats to 350. The restaurant averages a thousand guests a day, most of whom come for the mutton, but almost all of whom come for the all-you-can-eat buffet, a rarity in the world of barbecue restaurants.

SMOKED LAMB MEAT LOAF

The first time I tried smoked meat loaf was at Oak and Embers Tavern, a barbecue joint outside of Cleveland. I thought it was such a great idea that I decided to give it a try at home. That restaurant used a pretty traditional meat loaf recipe, but I went a different route. Since I was already planning to smoke a couple of whole lambs, I decided to break one of them down into ground lamb, using some for sausage and the rest for smoked lamb meat loaf. The results were phenomenal, and this recipe has become one of my backyard staples. Don't worry, you don't have to break down a whole lamb like I did—you can buy ground lamb at the grocery store! I love to serve this with Cucumber Salad (page 202) or Fireplace Potatoes (page 188).

2 pounds ground lamb

1 medium red onion, minced

4 garlic cloves, minced

1 serrano chile, stemmed, seeded, and minced

1 large egg, beaten

¼ cup tomato paste

¼ cup panko bread crumbs

1 teaspoon ground cinnamon

1 teaspoon ground cumin

1 teaspoon ground ginger

1 teaspoon hot paprika

1 teaspoon ground turmeric

½ cup fresh cilantro leaves, finely chopped

½ teaspoon kosher salt

½ teaspoon freshly ground black pepper

1. Prepare and preheat your smoker to 300°F.

2. In a large bowl, mix to combine the lamb, onion, garlic, chile, egg, tomato paste, bread crumbs, cinnamon, cumin, ginger, paprika, turmeric, cilantro, salt, and black pepper, being careful not to overwork the mixture. Set a large plate or quarter sheet pan on your work surface. Using your hands, form the meat into the shape of a bread loaf. Refrigerate for 1 hour.

3. When the temperature in the smoker reaches 300°F and the smoke is running clear, add the meat loaf directly onto the cooking grate. Cook until the meat loaf reaches an internal temperature of 160°F, about 1½ hours. For the best results, use a probe thermometer to continually monitor the meat's temperature.

4. Remove the meat loaf from the smoker, slice, and serve.

FIREPLACE LEG OF LAMB

After Kyle and I had mastered the Fireplace Chicken on a String (page 104) method and posted the results on Facebook, *The Chew* asked if I would bring Kyle on the show to prepare a leg of lamb together. It was fun to see that what started out as a little DIY project at home turned into Kyle's big national TV debut. He might have been a little shy right out of the gate, but since then he's been on the show several times and now is better than me in front of the camera!

6 shallots, minced

4 garlic cloves, minced

¼ cup chopped fresh rosemary

¼ cup chopped fresh oregano leaves

2 tablespoons sugar

2 tablespoons ground coriander

1 tablespoon crushed red pepper flakes

1½ tablespoons kosher salt

Butcher's twine

1 (6-pound) boneless leg of lamb

1. In a small bowl, mix to combine the shallots, garlic, rosemary, oregano, sugar, coriander, red pepper flakes, and salt. Pat the lamb dry with paper towels, season all sides with the spice mixture, cover, and refrigerate for several hours or up to overnight.

2. Build a nice big fire in a fireplace, fire pit, or grill.

3. Soak the butcher's twine in water, making sure to use enough for the suspension system (see pages 105–106 for instructions).

4. Allow the lamb to come to room temperature, about 1 hour. Tie up the lamb leg with the butcher's twine into a relatively even-width roast and suspend it from a hook in the ceiling or mantel so it hangs directly in front of the hottest part of the fire. Place a roasting pan beneath it to catch the drippings. Give the lamb a gentle twist so it slowly rotates as it cooks.

5. Every 20 minutes or so, moisten the twine with water to prevent it from igniting. If the lamb stops turning, give it another gentle twist. Continue feeding the fire to keep it hot. Cook until the lamb reaches an internal temperature of 140°F, about 3½ hours. Place a platter beneath the lamb, cut the twine, and let it rest for 30 minutes. Untie the lamb, slice, and serve with the hot drippings.

VEGETABLES
AND SIDES

GRILLED CORN
and Tomato Salad

When corn and tomatoes are at their absolute peak, this salad tastes like summer in a bowl. It goes great with pretty much any meat or fish you pull off the grill or out of the smoker. If you have any leftovers, gently heat them up and toss with pasta for an easy and amazing vegetarian meal. Soaking the ears overnight in salted water keeps the husks from going up in flames on the grill while adding a little bit of extra flavor.

4 ears sweet corn, unhusked

Kosher salt

1 garlic clove, minced

1 jalapeño, seeds and ribs removed, minced

Zest and juice of 3 limes

½ cup extra-virgin olive oil

1 ripe avocado, halved, pitted, peeled, and diced

1 cup halved cherry tomatoes

6 scallions, thinly sliced

¾ cup finely chopped fresh cilantro leaves

Freshly ground black pepper

1. Soak the corn in its husks in heavily salted water overnight in the refrigerator, keeping the ears submerged below the surface with a plate weighed down with a heavy can.

2. Prepare and preheat your lump charcoal grill to medium-low.

3. Put the corn, still in its husks, on the grill, cover, and cook for 20 minutes.

4. Meanwhile, in a large bowl, mix to combine the garlic, jalapeño, and a large pinch of salt. Add the lime zest, lime juice, and olive oil and whisk to combine. Add the avocado, tomatoes, scallions, and cilantro and toss gently to combine.

5. Remove the corn from the grill. When cool enough to handle, peel back the husks, discard the silk, and slice the kernels off the cobs directly into the bowl with a knife. Toss to combine. Season with salt and pepper.

SMOKED GREEN BEANS

Smoked green beans are kind of a staple all along the barbecue trail, where they offer a nice change of pace from tried-and-true baked beans. This recipe starts with the classic approach, but I give them a little bit of a French twist with the addition of amandine-style ingredients like Dijon mustard and crunchy slivered almonds.

1 teaspoon kosher salt, plus extra for blanching green beans

Ice

2 pounds green beans, ends trimmed

¼ cup slivered almonds

2 tablespoons Dijon mustard

1 tablespoon olive oil

1 tablespoon sherry vinegar

1. Prepare and preheat your smoker to 300°F.

2. Bring a large pot of salted water to a boil over high heat. Fill a large bowl with ice and water and set aside. Add the beans to the pot and cook for 45 seconds. Remove the beans and immediately plunge them into the ice-water bath to stop the cooking. Once they are cool, drain them and transfer to a paper towel–lined plate.

3. In a large bowl, combine the beans, almonds, mustard, olive oil, vinegar, and salt and toss to combine. Pour the bean mixture into a large casserole.

4. When the temperature in the smoker reaches 300°F and the smoke is running clear, add the beans and cook until they are nice and smoky, about 30 minutes. Serve.

SMOKED TOMATOES AND ONIONS

In late summer, I am absolutely swimming in juicy, garden-ripened tomatoes. I eat as many as possible fresh off the vine, but I'm always looking for other ways to use and preserve them. This is one of my favorites because I can use some immediately as a sauce or side to grilled or smoked meats, but also freeze some for the middle of winter when I'm missing my garden. I prefer firm plum tomatoes in this recipe because they hold up better than other varieties, but any ripe in-season tomatoes will do.

3 pounds plum tomatoes, quartered

3 large red onions, quartered

8 garlic cloves, thinly sliced

1 tablespoon cumin seeds

1 tablespoon kosher salt

Zest and juice of 1 lime

1 tablespoon olive oil

1. Prepare and preheat your smoker to 225°F.

2. In a large bowl, toss to combine the tomatoes, onions, garlic, cumin, salt, lime zest, lime juice, and olive oil.

3. Place the tomato-onion mixture on a roasting rack positioned on a baking sheet. When the temperature in the smoker reaches 225°F and the smoke is running clear, put the baking sheet in the smoker and cook until the tomatoes are nice and smoky, about 1 hour.

4. Remove the tomato-onion mixture from the smoker and serve as is or blend or purée to a chunky saucelike consistency. Use immediately or store in the refrigerator in an airtight container for up to 3 days.

SMOKED CORN ON THE COB

Pretty much everybody loves sweet corn on the cob, but in the Midwest—the Corn Belt—it's practically a religion. In summer, when corn is at peak freshness, we prepare it literally hundreds of different ways to keep things interesting. If you have the smoker going, give this recipe a try. This is like a smoky version of Mexican *elote,* the popular street food of cheese-coated grilled corn on a stick. Try to find ears of corn with long stems to make them easier (and less messy) to eat!

1½ cups (3 sticks) unsalted butter, softened

Zest and juice of 1 lime, plus lime wedges for serving

1 jalapeño, minced

2 tablespoons grated Parmesan cheese

1 tablespoon kosher salt

6 ears sweet corn, unhusked

1. Prepare and preheat your smoker to 300°F.

2. In a medium bowl, mix to combine the butter, lime zest, lime juice, jalapeño, Parmesan, and salt. Peel back (but don't remove) the corn husks. Remove and discard the silks. Spread the butter mixture over the corn, dividing it evenly, and replace the husks.

3. When the temperature in the smoker reaches 300°F and the smoke is running clear, add the corn and cook until they are nice and smoky, about 45 minutes. Transfer the corn to a large platter and serve with lime wedges.

SMOKED BEETS
with Horseradish

When we opened Mabel's, we decided to have some fun with the sides—to really give them a bit of their own style. Because I love beets so much, this was the first recipe we worked on. Roasted beets with horseradish are amazing, but hitting them with a dose of smoke gives them a whole different dimension. The best part is that vegans, vegetarians, and plain-old vegetable lovers can enjoy this hearty side, while we meat-eaters are chowing down on our third serving of brisket!

6 medium red beets, scrubbed

Small bunch fresh thyme

4 garlic cloves, unpeeled, smashed

½ cup plus 2 tablespoons olive oil

Kosher salt and freshly ground black pepper

3 tablespoons sherry vinegar

2 tablespoons fresh orange juice

2 tablespoons honey

1 teaspoon Dijon mustard

1 tablespoon grated fresh horseradish, plus more for serving

1 bunch scallions, thinly sliced

Flaky sea salt, like Maldon

1. Preheat the oven to 325°F.

2. In a shallow baking dish, combine the beets, thyme, and garlic. Drizzle with the 2 tablespoons olive oil and season with kosher salt and pepper. Add ¼ inch of water, then cover the baking dish tightly with aluminum foil and roast until the beets are easily pierced with a knife, about 1 hour.

3. Remove the baking dish from the oven and uncover. When the beets are cool enough to handle, cut off the ends. Using a clean kitchen towel or paper towel, scrub off the skins and discard. Cut the beets into wedges and set aside.

4. Prepare and preheat your smoker to 225°F.

5. In a medium bowl, whisk to combine the vinegar, orange juice, honey, and mustard. While whisking, add the remaining ½ cup olive oil in a steady stream to form an emulsion. Season with kosher salt and pepper.

6. Place the beets on a flat roasting rack positioned on a baking sheet. When the temperature in the smoker reaches 225°F and the smoke is running clear, add the beets. Cook for 20 minutes. Remove from the smoker and allow to cool completely.

7. In a large bowl, combine the beets, horseradish, vinaigrette, and three-quarters of the scallions and toss to combine. Season with sea salt. Serve on a platter and garnish with the remaining scallions and more grated fresh horseradish.

SERVES 6

SMOKY EGGPLANT DIP

If I have eggplants and I'm building a fire of any kind, I'm probably making this amazing dip. A twist on baba ghanoush, this recipe swaps the tahini for cool and creamy yogurt, which I always have on hand. I was nervous the first time I placed food directly into the coals of a fire, but now I do it all the time with everything from onions and beets to corn and potatoes. Make a batch of this to use as a dip with warm pita, an appetizer on a buffet, or a late-night snack. It will keep for a week in the fridge. If you're not familiar with za'atar, it's a nutty Middle Eastern spice blend that includes thyme, sesame seeds, and sumac.

3 medium eggplants

1 cup plain Greek yogurt

6 tablespoons olive oil, plus more for drizzling

Zest and juice of 1 lemon

1½ teaspoons kosher salt

½ teaspoon za'atar spice, plus more for garnish

Sumac, for serving (optional)

Grilled pita bread, for serving

1. Build a nice big wood fire in a fireplace, fire pit, or grill.

2. When the wood has burned down to a nice hot bed of glowing embers, place the eggplants directly into the coals. Cook, turning frequently, until deeply charred on all sides and soft, about 12 minutes. Remove from the coals and set aside.

3. When the eggplants are cool enough to handle, use a spoon to scoop out the flesh. Put the eggplant flesh in a food processor, add the yogurt, olive oil, lemon zest, lemon juice, salt, and za'atar and purée until smooth. Drizzle the finished purée with olive oil, garnish with the sumac (if using) and additional za'atar, and serve with the grilled pita bread.

SMOKY BUTTERNUT SQUASH
Purée

This is like the autumn version of the eggplant dip (page 181) that I make all summer long. The technique is pretty much the same—I toss the squash right into the hot coals—but hard winter squash takes much longer to cook. This is great as a snack dip or an accompaniment to roasted meats, but you can also turn it into comforting cold-weather soup by thinning it out with some hot vegetable stock or chicken stock.

½ cup olive oil

Small bunch fresh sage leaves, plus 4 leaves, finely chopped

1 teaspoon kosher salt, plus extra for frying sage leaves

1 teaspoon freshly ground black pepper, plus extra for frying sage leaves

2 medium butternut squash

1 garlic clove, minced

½ cup cider vinegar

½ cup crème fraîche

½ teaspoon grated nutmeg (preferably freshly grated)

1. Build a nice big wood fire in a fireplace, fire pit, or grill.

2. Put a small skillet over medium-high heat and add ¼ cup of the olive oil. When the oil is hot, carefully add the sage leaves and fry until crispy, about 5 seconds. Remove using a slotted spoon and drain on a paper towel–lined plate. Season with salt and pepper and set aside until needed.

3. When the wood has burned down to a nice hot bed of glowing embers, place the squash directly into the coals. Cook, turning frequently, until deeply charred on all sides and soft, about 1 hour. Remove from the coals and set aside.

4. When the squash is cool enough to handle, halve it, discard the seeds, and scoop out the flesh with a spoon (discard the skin). Put the squash flesh in a food processor, add the garlic, chopped sage, vinegar, crème fraîche, salt, pepper, and nutmeg and purée until smooth. Drizzle the finished purée with the remaining ¼ cup olive oil, garnish with the crispy sage leaves, and serve.

FIREPLACE ROOT VEGETABLES

This is one of Lizzie's favorite side dishes. I usually make it alongside fireplace chicken (page 104) since we already have a nice fire going. I start them under the chicken so they catch some of the amazing schmaltz drippings before popping them directly onto the embers in the fireplace to finish roasting. We are addicted to chestnut honey, a dark and smoky variety, but any good raw honey will work.

2 pounds carrots, cut crosswise into 1-inch pieces

2 pounds parsnips, cut crosswise into 1-inch pieces

2 pounds turnips, peeled and cut into 1-inch pieces

1 small red onion, halved and sliced

2 garlic cloves, minced

¼ cup finely chopped fresh thyme leaves

Juice of 2 oranges

2 tablespoons chestnut honey or good-quality raw honey

¼ cup olive oil

1 teaspoon kosher salt

1 teaspoon smoked paprika

1. Build a nice big wood fire in a fireplace, fire pit, or grill.

2. In a large bowl, combine all the ingredients and toss thoroughly. Put the vegetables in a single layer in a large cast-iron pan.

3. When the wood has burned down to a nice hot bed of glowing embers, place the cast-iron pan directly on top of the hot coals. Roast the vegetables, stirring occasionally, until they are slightly tender and very deeply caramelized, about 1 hour. Transfer to a platter and serve.

FIREPLACE POTATOES

This recipe is based on the Greek-style potatoes that my family always serves with lamb. They definitely go great with Grilled Lamb Shoulder Avgolemono (page 158) and Fireplace Leg of Lamb (page 167), but there's no reason not to make them when you're making Fireplace Chicken on a String (page 104), either. I love the amazing crust that forms on the spuds from the hot cast-iron pan.

4 pounds whole fingerling or baby red potatoes, washed

1 lemon, thinly sliced into rounds

5 sprigs fresh rosemary (on the stem)

Olive oil

Kosher salt and freshly ground black pepper

1. Build a nice big fire in a fireplace, fire pit, or grill.

2. In a large cast-iron pan, combine the potatoes, lemon slices, and rosemary. Drizzle with olive oil and season liberally with salt and pepper. When you have a nice hot bed of embers, place the cast-iron pan directly on top of the hot coals. Roast the potatoes, stirring occasionally, until they are tender and very deeply caramelized, about 1 hour. Serve.

SPAETZLE AND CABBAGE

This recipe is based on the wonderfully comforting Polish dish *haluski,* which combines sautéed cabbage and egg noodles. The best versions replace the egg noodles with nubby little spaetzle, and the added effort and time it takes to make them from scratch is worth it. Together, humble ingredients like cabbage, onion, butter, and noodles combine to create a truly amazing side dish. I love serving this dish with any smoked meat, but especially pork and sausage.

4 large eggs

½ cup whole milk

2 tablespoons Dijon mustard

Kosher salt and freshly ground black pepper

3 cups all-purpose flour

4 tablespoons (½ stick) unsalted butter

1 yellow onion, halved and diced

1 head green cabbage, halved, cored, and sliced

1 tablespoon finely chopped fresh flat-leaf parsley leaves

1. In a large bowl, whisk to combine the eggs, milk and mustard. Season well with salt and pepper. Add the flour and stir to form a sticky batter. Cover and refrigerate for up to 2 hours.

2. Put a large skillet over medium heat. Add the butter, onion, and a pinch of salt. Cook until the onion is soft and translucent, stirring occasionally, about 10 minutes. Add the cabbage and stir to combine. Add another pinch of salt and some pepper and cook until the cabbage is soft, about 5 minutes.

3. Meanwhile, bring a large pot of salted water to a boil. Lightly dampen a cutting board. Using a moistened rubber spatula, spread the chilled batter into a 2-inch-thick ribbon down the middle of the dampened board. Holding the cutting board over the edge of the pot, quickly cut and slide ¼-inch-wide pieces of the batter into the boiling water using a knife or bench scraper (you may have to cook the spaetzle in batches so as not to overcrowd the pot). When the spaetzle floats, after about 1 minute, cook for 30 seconds more. Remove the spaetzle from the water with a slotted spoon and add it to the cabbage mixture.

4. Stir to combine, garnish with the parsley, and serve.

SPICY GREENS

I love Southern-style braised collard greens, but sometimes I like to switch things up. Any number of hearty leafy greens like kale, Swiss chard, mustard greens, and even beet tops work great in this recipe, but I love the mildly bitter bite of escarole—which is related to endive—best.

1 tablespoon olive oil

½ pound thick-cut bacon, cut into large dice

2 medium yellow onions, halved and cut into large dice

4 garlic cloves, thinly sliced

2½ pounds escarole, cored and coarsely chopped

½ teaspoon crushed red pepper flakes

Kosher salt

¼ cup red wine vinegar

1 teaspoon sugar

Freshly ground black pepper

Hot sauce (optional)

1. In a large Dutch oven, heat the olive oil over medium heat. Add the bacon and cook, stirring occasionally, until crisp, about 5 minutes. Add the onions and garlic and cook until the vegetables soften, about 3 minutes. Add the escarole, red pepper flakes, and a large pinch of salt. If the greens don't all fit at once, add them to the pot in batches, waiting for some of the greens to wilt to add more. Cover, reduce the heat to medium-low, and cook until all the escarole begins to wilt, about 5 minutes.

2. Add the vinegar and sugar, replace the cover, and cook for 15 minutes. Remove from the heat and taste and adjust the seasoning, adding salt and black pepper as needed. If the greens are not spicy enough, add your favorite hot sauce. Serve.

BRISKET BAKED LIMA BEANS

When trimming a brisket (page 79) fresh out of the smoker, I always set aside the dark, crunchy, and fatty bits for another use, like Brisket Melts (page 86) or this amazing dish. The only way to improve upon a big crock of limas braised with bacon, beer, bourbon, and brown sugar is to add the ultimate "B" food: brisket!

1 pound dried giant lima beans

1 tablespoon olive oil

¼ pound slab bacon, cut into large dice

1 yellow onion, cut into large dice

1 jalapeño, thinly sliced into rings

2 teaspoons sweet paprika

2 tablespoons tomato paste

2 tablespoons Bertman Ball Park Mustard or other brown stadium-style mustard

3 tablespoons packed light brown sugar

¼ cup dark molasses

1 (12-ounce) bottle lager-style beer

½ cup cider vinegar

¼ cup bourbon

Kosher salt and freshly ground black pepper

½ pound burnt ends or brisket trimmings

1. The night before preparation, put the beans in a large bowl and cover with cold water by at least 4 inches. Refrigerate overnight.

2. Drain the beans, reserving 2½ cups of the soaking liquid.

3. In a large Dutch oven, heat the olive oil over medium heat. Add the bacon and cook, stirring occasionally, until crisp, about 5 minutes. Add the onion and jalapeño and cook, stirring occasionally, until soft, about 2 minutes. Reduce the heat to medium-low, add the paprika, tomato paste, mustard, brown sugar, and molasses and stir to combine.

4. Add the soaked beans, beer, vinegar, bourbon, and the reserved soaking liquid and stir to combine. Reduce the heat to low, cover, and cook, stirring occasionally, until the beans are very tender and the liquid has reduced and thickened slightly, about 3½ hours. Season with salt and black pepper. Stir in the brisket and serve.

JW POTATOES,
Mabel's Style

I am a french-fry fanatic, but the first time I tasted chef Jonathan Waxman's crispy fried potatoes, I knew I could never go back to plain old spuds. By a mile, his are the best fried potatoes you'll ever pop into your mouth. Ours come close, because we modeled them after JW's—hey, if you can't beat 'em, join 'em! We give them a slight twist at the end—toss them in a sherry vinaigrette—to make them our own. Like the originals, these golden nuggets of bliss have the perfect contrast of crunchy exterior and creamy core, and the rough and crunchy exterior is great for grabbing the bright and tangy vinaigrette.

3 large skin-on russet potatoes

3 tablespoons Dijon mustard

¼ cup sherry vinegar

⅓ cup olive oil

Peanut oil or lard, for frying

½ cup thinly sliced scallions

Flaky sea salt, like Maldon

1. Preheat the oven to 400°F.

2. Scrub the potatoes, place them on a baking sheet, and bake until the thickest part is easily pierced with a knife, about 1 hour 15 minutes. Remove the pan from the oven and allow to cool completely. When the potatoes are cool enough to handle, break them up by hand into rough 1- or 2-inch pieces. (This step can be done a day in advance; refrigerate the potatoes until needed.)

3. In a small bowl, whisk to combine the mustard and vinegar. While whisking, add the olive oil in a steady stream to form an emulsion.

4. In a deep fryer or pot over medium-high heat, heat about 4 inches of oil or lard to 360°F. Fry the potatoes in batches until golden brown and crisp, using a slotted spoon or frying spider to turn them often, about 4 minutes. When done, use a slotted spoon to transfer the fried potatoes to a paper towel–lined plate.

5. In a large bowl, combine the potatoes, scallions, and enough vinaigrette to lightly coat and toss to combine. Pour onto a platter, sprinkle with flaky salt, and serve immediately.

I'm very proud of the style of barbecue that we introduced to Clevelanders at Mabel's. Nothing makes me happier than seeing groups of people sitting around a big table in the restaurant and enjoying a style of food that truly represents them.

SERVES 6

SPICY POTATO GRATIN

Who doesn't love cheesy baked potato casseroles? This version spices things up a bit by using smoky chipotles in adobo sauce and fragrant Gruyère in the cheese sauce. Because a crunchy topping is just about mandatory, I sprinkle the whole thing with crispy panko bread crumbs. A mandoline will make quick work of slicing the potatoes.

2 tablespoons unsalted butter, plus extra for greasing the baking dish

3 tablespoons all-purpose flour

2½ cups whole milk

Kosher salt and freshly ground black pepper

½ teaspoon grated nutmeg (preferably freshly grated)

1½ cups shredded Gruyère cheese

2 tablespoons puréed chipotles in adobo sauce (see Note, page 92)

3 pounds russet potatoes, peeled and sliced crosswise ⅛ inch thick

¼ cup panko bread crumbs

1. Preheat the oven to 375°F. Grease a large casserole dish with some butter.

2. In a saucepan, melt the butter over medium-high heat. Whisk in the flour to form a smooth paste. While whisking, slowly add the milk in a steady stream to form a smooth sauce. Bring the sauce to a simmer, whisking to prevent the formation of any lumps (be sure to get into the corners of the pan so nothing burns). Season with salt and pepper. Add the nutmeg and cheese, whisking until thick and smooth. Whisk in the puréed chipotles.

3. Put the potatoes in a large bowl and season with salt and pepper. Pour in the cheese sauce and toss to thoroughly coat the potatoes. Evenly arrange the potatoes in the greased casserole dish, sprinkle with the bread crumbs, and cover tightly with aluminum foil.

4. Bake until the potatoes are easily pierced with a knife, about 1 hour. Uncover and bake until the top is golden brown and crisp, about 15 minutes. Remove from the oven and let sit for 10 minutes before serving.

SERVES 4

CUCUMBER SALAD

Growing up in the Midwest, pretty much every summer "barbecue" looked and tasted the same. There were the large plastic-tablecloth-covered card tables in the garage, the keg or coolers filled with light beer, and the assortment of overcooked hamburgers and excessively charred hot dogs. But there was also this refreshing cucumber salad, which managed to make everything else taste better. Loaded with fresh dill, crunchy onions, and tangy sour cream, this side will always be one of my favorites (which is why I serve it at Mabel's).

½ cup sour cream

1 tablespoon white wine vinegar

3 tablespoons chopped fresh dill

1 English cucumber, sliced into ⅛-inch-thick rounds

½ medium red onion, thinly sliced

Kosher salt and freshly ground black pepper

1. In a large bowl, whisk to combine the sour cream, vinegar, and dill. Add the cucumber and red onion, season with salt and pepper, and toss to combine.

2. Eat immediately or wrap tightly with plastic wrap and refrigerate for up to 1 week.

POPPY SEED COLESLAW

Almost every sports fan who grew up in Cleveland loves mustard. That's because as kids we all went to Cleveland Municipal Stadium to watch the Indians and the Browns play, and while we were there we scarfed down countless hot dogs covered with Bertman Ball Park Mustard. The unique flavor of that brown, spicy condiment stirs such powerful memories for so many people that we find a million different ways to use it. The addition of nutty, crunchy poppy seeds adds a fun visual appeal and a nice texture.

½ cup cider vinegar

½ cup sugar

2 tablespoons mayonnaise

2 tablespoons Bertman Ball Park Mustard or other brown stadium-style mustard

2 tablespoons poppy seeds

1 cup olive oil

Kosher salt and freshly ground black pepper

6 cups thickly shredded green cabbage

6 cups thickly shredded red cabbage

1 small red onion, halved and thinly sliced

1 cup roughly torn fresh cilantro leaves

1. In a large bowl, whisk to combine the vinegar, sugar, mayonnaise, mustard, and poppy seeds. While whisking, add the olive oil in a steady stream to form an emulsion. Season with salt and pepper.

2. Fold in the green and red cabbage, onion, and cilantro. Taste and adjust the seasoning, adding salt and pepper as needed. Serve immediately or refrigerate in an airtight container for up to 1 day before serving.

SAUERKRAUT

Sauerkraut is a magical food. Through the simple process of fermentation, regular old cabbage and salt transform into one of the world's most popular accompaniments to roasted and smoked meats. Sauerkraut goes great on hot dogs and brats, but also on burgers, pierogies, and even pizza! And it is super beneficial to your health—bonus!

2 large heads green cabbage

¼ cup kosher salt

1 tablespoon caraway seeds

1. Quarter and core both heads of cabbage. Cut the cabbage into ⅛-inch-wide strips, rinse under cold water, and drain. In a very large bowl, combine the cabbage and the salt and massage the cabbage until it begins to wilt, about 3 minutes. Add the caraway seeds and toss to combine. Set aside until you see liquid begin to accumulate in the bottom of the bowl, about 15 minutes.

2. Tightly pack the cabbage with its liquid into two clean quart-size mason jars, leaving 2 inches of air space at the top. Place a water-filled glass in the jar and press it down on top of the cabbage to keep it submerged below the surface of the liquid. Let it sit like this in a cool, dark, dry space to ferment for 7 to 10 days. Every few days, press down on the glass to keep the cabbage submerged below the surface of the liquid. The longer the sauerkraut ferments, the sourer it will get. Use immediately or store in the refrigerator for up to 1 month.

BRUSSELS SPROUT
and Apple Slaw

This crunchy, refreshing slaw goes great with almost any type of grilled or smoked meat. Sweet honey softens the tartness of the green apple, while the mustard adds comforting depth and complexity. I recommend using a mandoline to thinly shave the brussels sprouts, but a sharp knife and a steady hand works, too.

1 teaspoon cumin seeds

1 tablespoon honey

1 tablespoon Dijon mustard

3 tablespoons sherry vinegar

¼ cup olive oil

Kosher salt and freshly ground black pepper

1 pound brussels sprouts, ends removed and very thinly sliced

1 Granny Smith apple, halved, cored, and cut into matchsticks (I like to leave the peel on)

1 cup finely chopped fresh flat-leaf parsley

4 scallions, thinly sliced

1. Put a small skillet over medium heat. Add the cumin seeds and toast until lightly golden brown and fragrant, about 2 minutes. Remove from the heat.

2. In a medium bowl, whisk to combine the toasted cumin seeds, honey, mustard, and vinegar. While whisking, add the olive oil in a steady stream to form an emulsion. Season with salt and pepper. Add the brussels sprouts, apple, parsley, and scallions and toss to combine. Taste and adjust the seasoning, adding salt and pepper as needed. Serve immediately (the apples will brown the longer they sit out).

BROCCOLI SALAD

Growing up, it wasn't a summer barbecue without crunchy broccoli salad. Moms everywhere tricked their kids into eating green vegetables by coating broccoli in a sweet and creamy dressing and tossing it with tart cherries and crunchy peanuts. It's a great no-cook salad for hot summer months and is one of the most popular side dishes at Mabel's—for both adults and children!

¾ cup plain Greek yogurt

1 cup buttermilk

¼ cup cider vinegar

2 tablespoons packed light brown sugar

1 tablespoon Bertman Ball Park Mustard or other brown stadium-style mustard

1 teaspoon grated nutmeg (preferably freshly grated)

½ cup finely chopped fresh dill, plus additional sprigs for serving

Kosher salt and freshly ground black pepper

1 large bunch broccoli, cut into small florets, stems peeled, quartered lengthwise, and thinly sliced

1 cup roasted salted peanuts

1 cup dried cherries

1 cup thinly sliced scallions

1. In a large bowl, whisk to combine the yogurt, buttermilk, vinegar, brown sugar, mustard, nutmeg, and dill. Season with salt and pepper. Stir in the broccoli, peanuts, cherries, and scallions.

2. Taste and adjust the seasoning, adding salt and pepper as needed. Serve immediately topped with dill sprigs or refrigerate for up to 1 day before serving.

CELERY ROOT SLAW

Celery root might look all knobby and weird, but it has a delightfully earthy, grassy flavor with subtle and pleasant aromas of celery. This crispy, crunchy slaw allows those flavors to shine thanks to a simple vinaigrette and some fresh herbs. It's especially great served alongside grilled chicken.

1 small shallot, minced

Zest and juice of 2 lemons

1 teaspoon Dijon mustard

½ cup olive oil

Kosher salt and freshly ground black pepper

2 medium celery roots (about 1½ pounds), peeled and cut into matchsticks

½ cup finely chopped fresh tarragon leaves

½ cup finely chopped fresh flat-leaf parsley (optional)

In a large bowl, whisk to combine the shallot, lemon zest, lemon juice, and mustard. While whisking, add the olive oil in a steady stream to form an emulsion. Season with salt and pepper. Stir in the celery root, tarragon, and parsley (if using). Taste and adjust the seasoning, adding salt and pepper as needed. Serve immediately or refrigerate in an airtight container for up to 1 day before serving.

SHAVED CARROT SALAD

An amazing thing happens to carrots when you shave them into long ribbons. Not only are they gorgeous to look at—especially if you use carrots of different colors—but the texture softens to a gentle crunch. Use a mandoline or sharp vegetable peeler to form long, thin strips. Fresh mint really gives this salad a summery boost.

2 teaspoons cumin seeds

¼ cup red wine vinegar

1 tablespoon honey

¼ cup olive oil

Kosher salt and freshly ground black pepper

1 pound carrots, shaved into long ribbons

4 scallions, thinly sliced

1 cup finely chopped fresh mint leaves

⅔ cup coarsely chopped roasted salted peanuts

1. Put a small skillet over medium heat. Add the cumin seeds and toast until lightly golden brown and fragrant, about 2 minutes. Remove from the heat.

2. In a medium bowl, whisk to combine the toasted cumin seeds, vinegar, and honey. While whisking, add the olive oil in a steady stream to form an emulsion. Season with salt and pepper. Add the carrots, scallions, mint, and peanuts and toss to combine. Taste and adjust the seasoning, adding salt and pepper as needed. Serve immediately or refrigerate in an airtight container for up to 1 day before serving.

SHAVED CAULIFLOWER SALAD

Most of us shy away from raw cauliflower unless it's part of a veggie tray and it's dipped deep into ranch dressing. This fresh and easy salad will make converts out of all the doubters. Shaved thinly, the cauliflower tastes almost like shredded cabbage and, when tossed with the honey-sweetened vinaigrette, becomes a uniquely flavored and versatile side to just about any grilled or smoked food. Mild white anchovies add a pleasant brininess while the nuts pack a crunchy punch.

2 tablespoons sherry vinegar

1 teaspoon honey

2 white anchovies, mashed with a fork

¼ cup olive oil

Kosher salt and freshly ground black pepper

1 large cauliflower, quartered and cored

½ cup coarsely chopped toasted macadamia nuts

1 cup finely chopped fresh flat-leaf parsley

1. In a small bowl, whisk to combine the vinegar, honey, and anchovies. While whisking, add the olive oil in a steady stream to form an emulsion. Season with salt and pepper.

2. Using a mandoline or sharp knife, shave the cauliflower quarters into very thin pieces. If some small florets break off (and they will), just toss them into the bowl. In a large bowl, combine the shaved cauliflower, macadamia nuts, parsley, and vinaigrette and toss to combine. Season with salt and pepper. Serve immediately or refrigerate in an airtight container for up to 1 day before serving.

BBQ SAUCES, RELISHES, AND RUBS

CLEVELAND BBQ SAUCE

When I first told people about my plan to prepare "Cleveland-style" barbecue at Mabel's, I got a lot of skeptical looks. The responses ranged from things like "Do we really need a new style of barbecue?" to "Does Cleveland even have a barbecue culture?" What I wanted to do was combine generations of classic barbecue techniques from across the country with Northeast Ohio hardwoods, foods, spices, and flavors to create something completely new and unique. Like our signature barbecue sauce, which stars local legend Bertman Ball Park Mustard. Baste grilled foods with sauce only during the final stages of grilling to prevent the sugars in the sauce from burning.

2 cups cider vinegar

1 small red onion, quartered

1 large garlic clove, smashed

1 chipotle in adobo sauce, plus 1 tablespoon of sauce from the can

3 tablespoons bourbon

1 teaspoon coriander seeds

½ teaspoon smoked paprika

1 cup Bertman Ball Park Mustard or other brown stadium-style mustard

½ cup yellow mustard

¼ cup pure maple syrup

1 tablespoon soy sauce

2 teaspoons kosher salt

1½ teaspoons freshly ground black pepper

1. In a medium saucepan, combine the vinegar, onion, garlic, chipotle in adobo, bourbon, coriander, and paprika. Bring to a gentle boil over medium-high heat, then reduce the heat to medium-low and simmer until the flavors come together, about 10 minutes.

2. Meanwhile, in a medium bowl, whisk together the chipotle purée, brown and yellow mustards, maple syrup, soy sauce, salt, and pepper. Strain the vinegar mixture through a fine-mesh sieve into the mustard mixture (discard the solids) and whisk until smooth and combined.

3. Use immediately or store in the refrigerator in an airtight container for up to 1 month.

Kansas City
BBQ Sauce

Carolina
BBQ Sauce

Texas
BBQ Sauce

Memphis
BBQ Sauce

Cleveland
BBQ Sauce

CAROLINA BBQ SAUCE

If I'm going whole hog or making pulled or chopped pork, I'm whipping up a batch of this Carolina barbecue sauce. Nothing goes better with slow-cooked pork than a tangy vinegar-and-mustard-based sauce like this one.

2 cups yellow mustard

1 tablespoon tomato paste

2 tablespoons puréed chipotles in adobo (see Note, page 92)

⅔ cup packed light brown sugar

8 ounces (1 cup) lager-style beer

¼ cup cider vinegar

¼ cup distilled white vinegar

3 tablespoons Worcestershire sauce

½ teaspoon cayenne pepper

½ teaspoon freshly ground black pepper

Kosher salt

1. In a medium nonreactive saucepan, combine the mustard, tomato paste, chipotle purée, sugar, beer, cider vinegar, white vinegar, Worcestershire sauce, cayenne, black pepper, and salt to taste, whisking to combine. Bring the mixture to a boil over medium-high heat, reduce the heat to low, and simmer, stirring occasionally, until the flavors come together and the sauce thickens slightly, about 20 minutes.

2. Use immediately or store in the refrigerator for up to 1 month. (Baste grilled foods with sauce only during the final stages of grilling to prevent the sugars in the sauce from burning.)

KANSAS CITY BBQ SAUCE

Kansas City barbecue sauce leans to the sweeter side of things, thanks to healthy amounts of brown sugar, molasses, and tomato sauce. This sauce is the natural partner for beefy burnt ends but also slabs of meaty pork ribs.

3 tablespoons unsalted butter

1 small yellow onion, halved and finely diced

3 garlic cloves, minced

Kosher salt

2 cups tomato sauce

½ cup packed light brown sugar

⅓ cup cider vinegar

⅓ cup dark molasses

¼ cup tomato paste

3 tablespoons yellow mustard

1 tablespoon chili powder

½ teaspoon cayenne pepper

Freshly ground black pepper

1. In a medium nonreactive saucepan, melt the butter over medium heat. Add the onion, garlic, and a pinch of salt and cook, stirring occasionally, until the onion is tender, about 5 minutes. Reduce the heat to medium-low and add the tomato sauce, brown sugar, vinegar, molasses, tomato paste, mustard, chili powder, and cayenne, whisking to combine. Season with salt and black pepper. Bring to a gentle simmer and cook, stirring occasionally, until the flavors come together, about 30 minutes. Remove from the heat and carefully blend or purée until smooth.

2. Use immediately or store in the refrigerator in an airtight container for up to 1 month. (Baste grilled foods with sauce only during the final stages of grilling to prevent the sugars in the sauce from burning.)

MEMPHIS BBQ SAUCE

Like Kansas City barbecue sauce, Memphis style runs a bit sweeter than others, thanks to brown sugar and molasses. But it is also thinner and tangier, making it a great finishing baste or dipping sauce to be served with Memphis dry rubs.

3 tablespoons unsalted butter

1 small onion, halved and finely diced

3 garlic cloves, minced

Kosher salt

2 cups tomato sauce

½ cup tomato paste

⅓ cup packed light brown sugar

⅓ cup dark molasses

3 tablespoons Worcestershire sauce

2 tablespoons yellow mustard

1½ teaspoons celery seeds

½ teaspoon crushed red pepper flakes

2 tablespoons cider vinegar

1. In a medium nonreactive saucepan, melt the butter over medium heat. Add the onion, garlic, and a pinch of salt and cook, stirring occasionally, until soft, about 5 minutes. Reduce the heat to medium-low and add the tomato sauce, tomato paste, brown sugar, molasses, Worcestershire sauce, mustard, celery seeds, and red pepper flakes, whisking to combine. Bring to a gentle simmer and cook, stirring occasionally, until the flavors come together, about 30 minutes. Remove from the heat and blend or purée until smooth. Stir in the vinegar.

2. Use immediately or store in the refrigerator in an airtight container for up to 1 month. (Baste grilled foods with sauce only during the final stages of grilling to prevent the sugars in the sauce from burning.)

CHRIS LILLY
Big Bob Gibson BBQ

SPECIALTY: Alabama-Style White Barbecue Sauce

Down in Alabama, they do barbecue a little differently than the neighbors do. According to Chris Lilly, fifth-generation owner of the iconic Big Bob Gibson BBQ in Decatur, the name of the game is whole pork shoulders and whole split chickens slow smoked over local hickory wood. If that sounds pretty conventional, consider that one of the most ubiquitous barbecue sauces in that region is white.

"People who were raised in Decatur generally think barbecue sauce is supposed to be white," Lilly explains. "It's not until they get out and about that they realize white barbecue sauce is unique to Decatur."

Big Bob Gibson was Lilly's wife's great-grandfather, and all white barbecue sauces lead back to him, specifically to his backyard, where he first began his barbecue career in the early 1920s. As Lilly explains it, Gibson would slow smoke whole pork shoulders and split chickens in a hand-dug hickory pit for hours.

"He loved the Eastern Carolina–style vinegar-based mops, he loved the extra tang that it gave to all his barbecue, but he also needed a way to keep the whole chickens from drying out," says Lilly. "So he added mayonnaise, which took the edge off the vinegar while also adding fat back to the chicken to keep it from drying out."

All these years later, every chicken that comes off the pit at Big Bob Gibson BBQ gets dipped into a vat of white barbecue sauce. Every table is graced with a side of that world-famous white sauce, and bottles of the finger-licking elixir are purchased by the case for home consumption, where it is used as a baste, mop, dressing, and side sauce.

"At the restaurant, it goes on pork, it goes on chicken, it goes on turkey," Lilly reports. "They put it on their salads, dip their Golden Flake potato chips in it. Basically, it's a condiment for just about everything."

TEXAS BBQ SAUCE

Across vast stretches of Texas, many people don't even bother with barbecue sauce, rightly believing that great brisket requires nothing more than salt, pepper, and wood smoke to reach its beefy potential. That said, if I had to pick a sauce to pair with Texas-style brisket, it would be this one.

3 tablespoons unsalted butter

1 small onion, halved and finely diced

Kosher salt

1 tablespoon sweet paprika

1 teaspoon chili powder

2 cups tomato sauce

¼ cup tomato paste

⅓ cup dark molasses

¼ cup Worcestershire sauce

1 whole chipotle in adobo sauce

⅓ cup fresh lemon juice

Freshly ground black pepper

1. In a nonreactive medium saucepan, melt the butter over medium heat. Add the onion and a pinch of salt and cook, stirring occasionally, until soft, about 5 minutes. Reduce the heat to medium-low and add the paprika, chili powder, tomato sauce, tomato paste, molasses, Worcestershire sauce, and chipotle, whisking to combine. Bring to a gentle simmer and cook, stirring occasionally, until the flavors come together, about 30 minutes.

2. Remove from the heat and blend or purée until smooth. Stir in the lemon juice and season to taste with salt and pepper. Use immediately or store in the refrigerator for up to 1 month. (Baste grilled foods with sauce only during the final stages of grilling to prevent the sugars in the sauce from burning.)

PEPPER RELISH

Talk about delicious and versatile! This sweet, tangy, and complex bell pepper relish goes on almost everything, which is why I usually have a stash of it in my fridge all summer long. Try it on smoked or grilled meats, or as a garnish on charcuterie and cheese boards. It's amazing on sandwiches, and I even like it in my scrambled eggs! How's that for versatile?

2 red bell peppers, diced

2 yellow bell peppers, diced

2 green bell peppers, diced

2 jalapeños, minced

1 red onion, diced

2 garlic cloves, minced

Zest and juice of 1 orange

1 cup sherry vinegar

½ cup packed light brown sugar

1 tablespoon coriander seeds, toasted

1 tablespoon kosher salt

2 tablespoons finely chopped fresh flat-leaf parsley

1. In a large nonreactive saucepan, combine the bell peppers, jalapeños, onion, garlic, lime zest, lime juice, vinegar, brown sugar, coriander, and salt and bring to a simmer over medium heat. Cook, stirring occasionally, until all the liquid has evaporated and the mixture has thickened up, about 45 minutes.

2. Remove from the heat, allow to cool, and stir in the parsley.

3. Use immediately or store in the refrigerator for up to 1 month.

(Photograph on page 232)

Peach
Applesauce

Pepper Relish
(page 229)

PEACH APPLESAUCE

Applesauce is one of those foods that very few people bother to make at home because it's literally at every grocery store all the time. That's too bad because it is really easy to make and—no surprise here—the results are shockingly good. When I make it I usually toss in some other seasonal fruit, like pears in the fall or peaches in the summer. If those fruits are really ripe and sweet, you can even reduce (or eliminate altogether) the added sugar in this recipe.

6 Granny Smith apples, peeled and cored

6 ripe peaches, peeled and pitted

Zest and juice of 2 lemons

½ cup cider vinegar

½ cup packed light brown sugar

1 cinnamon stick

1 star anise pod

½ teaspoon ground allspice

1 teaspoon kosher salt

1. In a large nonreactive saucepan, combine the apples, peaches, lemon zest, lemon juice, vinegar, brown sugar, cinnamon stick, star anise, allspice, and salt and cook until the fruit is soft, about 1 hour. Remove and discard the cinnamon stick and star anise.

2. For a chunky applesauce, mash the mixture with a potato masher. If you prefer a smooth applesauce, blend or purée the mixture to the desired consistency.

3. Serve warm or cold. Use immediately or store in the refrigerator in an airtight container for up to 2 weeks.

OUR RUB RATIOS

At Mabel's, we often need to double, triple, or even quadruple rub recipes depending on the menu item, day of the week, or some other external factor like a home Cavs, Indians, or Browns game. That's why we prefer to use ratios instead of recipes. Because they rely on fixed proportions of ingredients relative to one another, they can easily be scaled up or down in quantity.

All these ratios are based on volume (tablespoons, cups) as opposed to weight. So, for example, if you were to base the Basic Rub ratios on 1 part equaling 1 cup, then you would combine 2 cups kosher salt with 2 cups freshly ground black pepper, ½ cup celery seeds, and ½ cup ground coriander. The total yield would be 5 cups. That's a lot of rub! For a smaller amount, do the same thing, basing 1 part on 1 tablespoon . . . you get the idea!

Basic Rub

2 parts kosher salt

2 parts freshly ground black pepper

½ part celery seed

½ part ground coriander

Pork Rub

5 parts Basic Rub

1 part sweet paprika

Beef Rib Rub

5 parts Basic Rub

½ part garlic powder

½ part yellow mustard seeds, coarsely ground

½ part sweet paprika

Lamb Rub

5 parts Basic Rub

1 part dried oregano

The book in your hands is the fifth cookbook that I've written in nine years; you'd think the process would have gotten easier by now! Each new project brings its own set of challenges and rewards, and *Playing with Fire* is no exception. But one thing remains constant: the amount of help and support I receive from a very wide circle of friends, family, and colleagues.

I wouldn't be here without Liz and Kyle, who are both so understanding about the excessive demands of work and travel. It was my mom, dad, and grandparents who all instilled in me not only a love of food, but a love of people, regardless of backgrounds. Our frequent family gatherings showed me how food has the power to strengthen bonds and friendships.

Thanks are due to my longtime friend, business partner, and golfing strategist Doug Petkovic, without whom I would have far fewer restaurants and many more golf balls!

Everybody who knows me recognizes that I wouldn't function properly without my dedicated and meticulous assistant, Rebecca Yody, who has been by my side since the beginning. Thanks for your bottomless support.

Thanks to Culinary Director Katie Pickens, whose painstaking testing guarantees that every recipe will come out great. Over the past decade, Katie has become like family to me and Liz. Corporate Chef Derek Clayton, my partner in crime, does all the heavy lifting and ensures that every plate in every restaurant is as good as or better than if I made it myself. Here's hoping that one day, my friend, your glass will be half-full! On the ground in Cleveland, Brad Ball, Dan Young, and Ryan Kasson—aka the Big Three—are honest-to-goodness masters of meat, who make smoked-meat dreams a reality each and every day at Mabel's BBQ.

Thanks to my manager of fifteen years, Scott Feldman of Two-Twelve Management, a real mensch who represents me as if I'm his only client and who understands the food and media business better than anybody. Thanks also to Jon Rosen and William Morris Agency, a team that always manages to ink the perfect deal. My longtime friend and PR wizard Becca Parrish, along with the rest of the folks at BeccaPR, always manage to paint the perfect picture.

My hilarious TV family at *The Chew* makes it feel like we're not even at work. I'm so fortunate to be a part of something so amazing.

This is the fourth book I've done with Douglas Trattner because he's a pleasure to work with and always manages to make me sound like I actually know what I'm talking about!

Photographer Ed Anderson, along with Andie McMahon and Devon Grimes, captured the mood and spirit of *Playing with Fire* while making every recipe look as delicious on the page as it does in real life. It was truly a once-in-a-lifetime honor to work with super-stylist Susan Spungen. She, with help from Catherine Yoo and Laura Kinsey Dolph, brought such a sharp eye and unique sense of style to the entire project. The book is so much better for it.

Raquel Pelzel, our editor at Clarkson Potter, might have come to this project midstream, but she carried us all to the finish line while keeping everybody on task and improving every detail.

And last, but not least, my heartfelt thanks go out to Kent Black of Black's Barbecue, Billy Durney of Hometown Bar-B-Que, Mike and Amy Mills of 17th Street Barbecue, Rodney Scott of Scott's Bar-B-Que, Samuel Jones of Skylight Inn BBQ, Pat Bosley of Moonlite Bar-B-Q, Carey Bringle of Peg Leg Porker, Patrick Martin of Martin's Bar-B-Que, Joe Pearce of Slap's BBQ, and Chris Lilly of Big Bob Gibson BBQ. You amazing pitmasters are an inspiration and have been so generous with your endless knowledge and continued support.

Published in the United States
by **CLARKSON POTTER/
PUBLISHERS,** an imprint of the
CROWN PUBLISHING GROUP,
a division of **PENGUIN RANDOM
HOUSE LLC,** New York.
crownpublishing.com
clarksonpotter.com

CLARKSON POTTER is a trademark
and **POTTER** with colophon is a
registered trademark of **PENGUIN
RANDOM HOUSE LLC.**

Library of Congress Cataloging-in-
Publication Data
Names: Symon, Michael, 1969–
author. | Trattner, Douglas, author.
Title: Michael Symon's playing with
fire / Michael Symon and Douglas
Trattner.
Other titles: Playing with fire
Description: First edition. | New York
Clarkson Potter/Publishers [2018]
Identifiers: LCCN 2017034644 |
ISBN 9780804186582 (hard cover) |
ISBN 9780804186599 (ebook)
Subjects: LCSH: Barbecuing. |
Cooking (Meat) | LCGFT: Cookbooks.
Classification: LCC TX840.B3
S96 2018 | DDC 641.7/6—dc23
LC record available at
https://lccn.loc.gov/2017034644

Printed in China

Book and cover design by
IAN DINGMAN
Cover photographs by
ED ANDERSON
Illustrations by **MORON EEL**

10 9 8 7 6 5 4 3 2 1

First edition

MICHAEL SYMON is a cohost of ABC's *The Chew* and Food Network's *Iron Chef America* and *Burgers, Brew & 'Que*. He is the chef and co-owner of the acclaimed restaurants Lola, Lolita, and Mabel's BBQ, all in Cleveland, Ohio; the B Spot burger restaurants throughout the Midwest; Roast in Detroit; Symon's Burger Joint in Austin, Texas; Bar Symon at airports in Pittsburgh and Washington, DC; and Angeline's at the Borgata in Atlantic City. He is the author of *Michael Symon's Live to Cook*, *Michael Symon's Carnivore*, *Michael Symon's 5 in 5*, and *Michael Symon's 5 in 5 for Every Season*.